LifeGivers Apologetics

Women Designed and Equipped to Share Reasons for the Hope Within

Tricia Scribner MAA, MSN

CONTENTS

Introduction 6

Part 1: Women Can Talk About the Hope Within

1: Women on the Front Lines of the Faith 10
2: Apologetics: You Were Made for This 16
3: Why Apologetics? 24
4: What is Apologetics? 33
5: Using Apologetics Wisely 39

Part 2: Talk About Truth

6: Truth on Trial 46
7: How We Know Things 52
8: The Boomerang Effect 58

Part 3: Talk About God

9: How You See It: What's a Worldview? 65
10: If Cause and Effect, Then God 70
11: If Order and Design, Then God 81
12: If Right and Wrong, Then God 93
13: If Evil, No God? 102
14: If God, Then Miracles 111

Part 4: Talk About Jesus

15: Can We Know What the New Testament Writers Wrote? 120
16: Were the New Testament Writers Who They Claimed to Be? . . 127
17: Were the New Testament Writers Trustworthy? The Internal
Evidence 133
18: Were the New Testament Writers Trustworthy? The External
Evidence 144
19: Did Jesus and His Disciples Believe He Was God? 154
20: Did Jesus Confirm His Deity by Fulfilling Old Testament
Prophecies? 162

21: Did Jesus' Life Bear Marks of Perfection and Miracles? 172
22: Did Jesus Physically Rise from the Dead? 180
23: Did Jesus Confirm the Bible Was God's Word? 186

Part 5: Talk to Walk Them to the Gospel

24: Preparing Ourselves for the Task Before Us 193
25: Cultivating Core Conversations 200
26: Sharing the Gospel Message 208

Endnotes

Endnotes 213

Acknowledgements

I have wanted for years to write an apologetics book focused on women. To have accomplished this goal is a great joy to me, and a goal I could not have met without the help of many people. To my precious group of apologetics-minded friends, Kim, Jennifer, Emily, Cyndi, and Linda, thank you for meeting with me weekly for months to hone your apologetics knowledge and skills. I cannot thank you enough for spurring me on to prepare apologetics resources designed for women. Linda, you have walked with me through the preparation of this manuscript, spending countless hours poring over the content, editing, encouraging, and fixing my numerous mistakes. What a friend.

My precious Sara, you fixed the copier, often checked on my progress, and spent hours taking pictures for my promotional materials. Sweet Emily, you edited my manuscript, giving me valuable feedback that helped me speak to the needs of young women. Neli dear, though you are far away in California, when we talk on the phone, you always encourage me. I love you, girls.

Randy, my sweetheart for 41 years, thank you for advising, investing in this work, and repeatedly fixing problems with my laptop. Mama, I am so glad you were visiting with us in the final days of manuscript preparation, praying with me and for me.

I also thank Frank Turek and Norman Geisler for their faithfulness to the Lord in ministry and for their influence on my understanding of apologetics and philosophical issues that bear upon our faith. Readers will find much of their thinking in these pages. It is understandable, as I studied under Dr. Geisler's tutelage at Southern Evangelical Seminary, and for eight years taught high school apologetics using their groundbreaking apologetics book, *I Don't Have Enough Faith to Be an Atheist*. In addition, Frank also has graciously given of his time to teach my high school students on our yearly apologetics field trip. I also appreciate his encouragement to get this book written, and his willingness to answer my questions about apologetics ministry.

Dearest Lord Jesus, I ask that you use the words in this book to equip women with the knowledge, confidence, and conviction that you are God in the flesh who came to earth and took the punishment for our sins, so that through faith in you we could have eternal life. I pray that Christian women will use this knowledge, not to win arguments, but to win souls for your kingdom. And I ask for the woman who may pick up this book in her search for truth, that she so clearly see you on every page that she trusts you to forgive her sins and to give her life eternal.

Introduction

God has called and equipped each member of His body uniquely. Some of us are good at numbers. I'm not one of those persons, but I'm glad I'm married to one, so that he can help me balance my checkbook. God has called some of us to the vocation of Christian philosophy and apologetics. I happen to be one of those persons. As a vocational apologist my job is to apply myself to learning so that I can explain more clearly the apologetics issues facing us as Christians in our everyday lives, as well as the evidence that Christianity reveals the most cogent, livable, and truthful answers to life's ultimate questions.

Dr. Daniel Wallace of the Center for the Study of New Testament Manuscripts makes a similar point:

> I have come to believe that Christian scholars have a duty to the church that we don't typically consider as part of our job description, vis., close the gap. How? By explaining in lay terms what all the scholarly fuss is about. By offering a different model, but one that is backed up with the best scholarship.[1]

His concern that Christian textual critics translate their knowledge of New Testament manuscripts to the laity is no less applicable to the area of apologetics.

I believe that it is a misunderstanding that some people are just so smart or have so much knowledge that they cannot explain their topic to the average person. This concerns me. I have found that for me the opposite is true. The more deeply I understand my topic, the better I am able to explain it in common language. Two educational ventures have helped me deepen my knowledge so that I can explain it more clearly to others. In seminary graduate school I recognized that I was just touching the tip of the iceberg in my studies, and this led me to continue my education. I also received a practical education when teaching high schoolers. Their perpetual, "But what about . . ?" kept me grappling with ways to explain abstract concepts. I still am not always successful and it troubles me deeply. I am pursuing further studies so that I can get better at it.

Though I do not see myself as a philosopher at heart, I recognize the need to understand philosophical principles undergirding my Christian faith, so that I can more clearly articulate truth. Now that my ministry focuses on women, I want to break down truths and share them clearly, so that the woman who is not a specialist in apologetics (just as I am not a specialist in accounting) can grab hold of the truths she needs in order to respond to her university professor, her friends, or her kids, as well as to help her find answers to her own faith questions. For this reason, I write this book for you, my precious Christian sister, whom I love through these pages.

It is my contention in this book that we as women are designed and called as physical and spiritual lifegivers. While I realize that in standard usage the word "life-givers" is hyphenated, I have chosen to coin a single compound word, which will be used throughout this book in order to illustrate lifegiving as a unified concept. By lifegiving I don't mean to imply that women are the ultimate lifegivers; only our God can do that. But He has uniquely designed women, and women alone, to participate in this unique endeavor.

As women, we share the truth of Christ because by nature we are designed for relationship and deeply care about those within our spheres of influence, as well as those whom God has placed in our personal care. Remember this motivation as you read this book.

Sometimes you may feel fearful, overwhelmed, or even confused by the information. I urge you to persevere. All worthy endeavors require effort and commitment. You don't have to learn *everything*. Be willing to learn *something*. When we don't understand what we are reading, we can mark it and revisit it. The struggle to understand is good. It cuts at the heart of our pride and provokes us to turn in humility to our Lord. Remember, the Spirit is working not only to build our knowledge, but also to transform our characters.

The reward for our efforts is immeasurably great. Imagine being able to respond to your co-worker who asks how you can believe that the New Testament is more than a fairy tale. Imagine being able to help your college-aged child not only survive spiritually, but even flourish in a course where the professor insists that the only people who believe in God are those who need a crutch to lean on. Imagine being rock-solid certain that your faith is well-placed in Jesus Christ, even when a co-worker insists that He is merely a good teacher, but not God.

The Lord promised that the Holy Spirit would help His apostles recall all that He said and did. The New Testament is the precious result of Jesus' promise. If we ask and yield ourselves to Him every time we open this book, we can be sure that the Lord will also help us understand and recall truths about Himself that He has embedded in the natural world.

To this end I have written this book. I hope you enjoy our journey together, as we explore the wonderful opportunity of answering the questions people ask about our faith, as we walk them to the gospel of Jesus Christ.

Part 1

Women Can Talk About the Hope Within

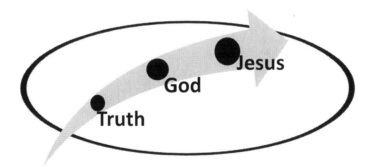

1

Women on the Front Lines of the Faith

I am a mom of three adult girls and "Nana" to six grandchildren. I have been married to Randy for 41 years. Currently I'm in a doctoral program and recently completed ten years of teaching apologetics in a Christian high school, so I'm daily steeped in the Christian worldview. But 35 years ago, while in my early twenties, I was slogging through nursing school courses that asserted claims about reality that were blatantly at odds with my Christian beliefs.

We were taught that as nurses we needed to be affirming, tolerant of the beliefs of all people, and never push our faith on patients. In anatomy and physiology class, the evolutionary model of the origin of life as well as that of complex life forms dominated, and believing the biblical account of the origin of man was considered naïve and backward. Upon graduation I worked as a public health nurse, which included family planning clinics where nurses provided birth control pills to patients, whether married or not.

I struggled with how to live out my faith and how to discern what was true. Among friends who were non-believers I was viewed as "religious" and even "fanatical," and through the years I wondered at times if maybe I just believed because I had been brought up that way.

Questions plagued me:
*How did I counter the view that the biblical account of creation, as well as many other historical narratives in the Bible, were just fairy tales?

*Were people essentially good when the Bible said that they were corrupt? How did I reconcile these two views? Could both be true?

*As a nurse, how did I minister to patients who were dying, given the professional expectation that I view all spiritual convictions as equally valid, and even though I believed there was only one source of real hope?

*What about evolution? Did the fossil evidence really support evolution? If not, then why did so many scientists believe it?

*As a person of science, I was supposed to base my treatment plans on the scientific evidence supporting the treatments and drugs that were effective. Given this view, how did Christianity stack up in terms of evidential support?

*Would I have to quit thinking and just rely on blind faith in order to stay Christian in my beliefs?

*Was faith really believing in something for which I had no evidence?

In addition to challenges from my professional life, I was also left mute by assertions from people of other faiths, such as a Jehovah's Witness who adamantly informed me that the word "Trinity" was nowhere in the Bible. Though I had been a believer in Jesus Christ since childhood, I had no idea what to say. This would not be the last time I would be caught off guard by those of other worldviews who seemed much better equipped than I to discuss the evidence for their faith. I was not ignorant of biblical teaching. I knew what I believed. I just didn't know the evidences supporting my belief.

In my desperation, I asked the hard questions. My pastor father helped me battle through some of them, and I fervently researched answers for myself. Finally, I came across Josh McDowell's *Evidence that Demands a Verdict*—the 1980s original version. That began my lifelong journey into apologetics, studying and sharing the evidences embedded in the world that show Christianity is true. Though at the time I did not know that I would enter the discipline of apologetics as a life's vocation, I was relieved to find that there was ample evidence available supporting Christian truth claims, and I devoured evidential support from a variety of sources.

Eventually my journey culminated in my leaving the nursing profession to pursue seminary studies in apologetics. I then started teaching apologetics in a Christian high school. Students regularly pummeled me with questions that troubled them. The daily grind of fielding questions forced me to think through my convictions and learn how to explain my rationale for these convictions. I noticed that even though the class of students changed each year, the kinds of questions did not. Certain common issues and objections cropped up repeatedly in our class discussions, which enabled me to become more proficient and confident in responding to concerns raised by my students.

Spiritual Foxholes

I've learned that my difficulties in answering questions about my faith were not unusual. We as Christian women live on the front lines of a spiritual battle in every season of our lives. Perhaps you will find something in common with one of the following women:

*Wanda's husband is agnostic. As an intellectual, her husband has often raised questions about how Wanda can be so sure that God exists. So far, all she can come up with is, "You just need to have faith." What Wanda doesn't know is that her husband's questions cover a deep concern and desire to know about God. Could it be that if she helped her husband resolve his questions about God's existence, he then would be open to the gospel message?

*Zoe lives in a college dorm with her roommate Aja, a Muslim. Aja has offered to show Zoe in the Bible where it prophesies the coming of the prophet Muhammad. She also has asked Zoe to explain how Christians can worship three Gods. Zoe has no idea how to answer her. She's afraid that maybe Aja is right, so she has quit talking about her faith completely.

*Maggie works at a hospital where she and other nurses will soon attend an in-service training on pain management techniques, such as therapeutic touch, biofeedback, and guided imagery. These treatments sound weird to her, and she wonders if these interventions conflict with her beliefs as a Christian. But she pushes aside her concern because she doesn't know that Christian apologists offer resources addressing these kinds of issues, and, after all, it's just part of her job.

*Elaine is a teacher, and tonight she will complete her lecture preparation on the origin of life for her Monday high school biology class. Though she is a Christian, her school does not permit the discussion of creation.

*Gina is mom to three children, ages 10, 13, and 18. Her 18-year-old son is headed to college next year, where the head professor of the religion department believes that the New Testament is a myth developed by second and third century church leaders. Gina has taken her children to church every Sunday since they were little, and her son is an active member of the student group. But Gina doesn't know that he is already reading articles online written by his skeptic, soon-to-be New Testament professor. Her son doesn't tell her because he doesn't want to her to know that he has major doubts about the trustworthiness of the New Testament.

*Karisa watches Oprah regularly because, though Karisa is a Christian, she appreciates Oprah's non-judgmental approach and interesting guests. Recently, Oprah insisted during one of her shows that there could not possibly be just one way to heaven or to whatever people want to call God. When Karisa recently shared her faith with a co-worker, the co-worker said that Karisa needed to be more tolerant. She wonders if maybe Christianity is too narrow-minded in claiming that it is the only way.

*When Margaret's friend, Elisa, went through a divorce, Elisa said that she wanted to be closer to God. So, Margaret shared the gospel, using Scripture. When she finished, Elisa asked, "If God loves me so much, why did He allow my husband to abandon me and my children for another woman? The God of the Bible just doesn't seem like a God I can lean on."

Like me, each of these women knows Christ as Savior. Each knows how to share the plan of salvation with someone using scriptures and various evangelistic formats. But what each is missing is knowing where to lead the conversation if the person raises questions about assertions made when sharing the gospel. Further, the faith of each of these women is at stake. I am not implying that she can lose her salvation, but she can certainly become spiritually crippled by doubts, and paralyzed when it comes to maturing in her faith and being an effective witness.

If Christian women are pressed on every side to explain why they believe in Christianity over all the religions of the world, if souls are at stake—their own, their children's, their neighbors' and co-workers'—, and if the lost from diverse religious backgrounds are asking good questions, then why aren't Christian women in local churches studying theology and apologetics as part of their own personal spiritual growth plans? Why aren't they preparing themselves to respond clearly and persuasively to questions, for the sake of Jesus Christ and for the lost whom He loves? Why aren't Christian bookstore shelves brimming with books that teach women how to talk to other women in everyday language about the foundations of our faith? Why aren't evangelical churches equipping women to engage intellectually with their culture—which is comprised of people, with homes and families, and souls?

While we may be tempted to blame publishers, bookstores, denominations, and churches, we as women must shoulder much of the responsibility ourselves. Publishers stay in business only if their books sell, as do bookstores. And churches develop programs in response to needs voiced by women themselves.

What subjects do Christian women want for their day-to-day reading, and what kinds of discipleship classes do they ask for? In my experience, few will join a group studying theological or apologetics topics. Generally speaking, we read practical self-help books that assist us in negotiating the challenges of everyday life, and we flock to meetings where entertainment and fellowship are high on the list of priorities.

Do not misunderstand. There are many godly women who pursue challenging Bible studies and meet regularly with groups that challenge and sharpen their thinking. But just as often, we as Christian women ignore the deeper theological and apologetics studies—what and why we believe—and busy ourselves studying man-made philosophies sprinkled with enough Christian-eze to keep us believing that we're spiritually maturing.

We have failed to heed the apostle Paul's admonition in Colossians 2:8: "See to it that no one takes you captive by philosophy and empty deceit, according to human tradition, according to the elemental spirits of the world, and not according to Christ." We also sometimes avoid studying anything that bites time out of our already over-booked schedules. Instead, we want an easy read or an uplifting but brief conference that ends in a giant group hug. Still, we chisel out time to get our hair highlighted, our nails painted, to watch our favorite TV shows, and to keep up with friends on social media. But we are just too busy to wear ourselves out loving God with our minds.

"I'm too busy," is a costly excuse. Our own spiritual maturing process calls for our pursuit of truth. Our children desperately need us to equip ourselves to respond to their questions. Our co-workers long for a Christian to give them some solid answers. And friends of other faiths wait to hear a clear explanation for why we believe that of all the worldviews Christianity provides the best explanation of reality.

The good news is, we can do this. We can think. We can think about these issues, we can apply ourselves to studying and learning the rational evidence supporting the truth claims of Christianity, and we can apply what we've learned in redemptive conversations. We not only can, we must. Eternity is on the line.

2

Apologetics: You Were Made for This

In order to understand why women make good apologists, we need to talk about how women are naturally designed. Despite what many in our culture tell us, men and women are different. Actually, they are complementary in design. When we study the creation narrative in Genesis 1 and 2, we learn God's plan for the family. We also discover how we can fulfill our design as men and women within the family unit, founded by the union of husband and wife. Genesis 1:26-28 describes God's design for man and woman:

> Then God said, "Let us make man in our image, after our likeness. And let them have dominion over the fish of the sea and over the birds of the heavens and over the livestock and over all the earth and over every creeping thing that creeps on the earth." So God created man in his own image, in the image of God he created him; male and female he created them. And God blessed them. And God said to them, "Be fruitful and multiply and fill the earth and subdue it, and have dominion over the fish of the sea and over the birds of the heavens and over every living thing that moves on the earth."

As far as our human nature and our value (ontologically), man and woman, and specifically, husband and wife, are created equal. Both are created in God's own likeness, both are given responsibility to rule the earth as God's on-site representatives, and both are commissioned to multiply.

In another sense, however, man and woman are clearly created distinct. Adam was created as leader of the family unit. The narrative itself confirms this. Man was created first, instructed to care for the garden (2:15), commanded to abstain from eating from the tree of the knowledge of good and evil (2:16), and also named the animals (2:19), all before woman was ever created.

Woman was created from man and presented to him by God (2:21-22), man even named the woman (2:23), and it was man who was commanded to leave his father and mother and cling to his wife, initiating and taking responsibility for a new family unit (Gen. 2:24). God's own actions in His creation of man reveal the husband's designated leadership role and also his naturally endowed inclination to care for and protect his wife.

We shouldn't think, however, that woman's design is any less unique and honorable. While functionally she is created as a helper to her husband and is to yield willingly to his leadership in the home, woman alone is endowed with the high and holy design and calling as lifegiver and life nurturer. By this I don't mean to attribute to woman some magical power or prestige, but simply to acknowledge that God specifically and uniquely designed woman for the role of conceiving, carrying, and bearing new life. This fact is acknowledged by Adam himself, who called his wife Eve, honoring her as the mother of all living (Gen. 3:20).

The fact that a specific woman may be single without children or married and unable to bear children, though she longs for them, doesn't change God's original design for woman. It is true that this broken world has produced brokenness within our physical bodies, preventing some of us from being able to bear children. But the very fact that we as women who desire children grieve deeply when we can't bear them, illustrates the truth that women are naturally designed as lifegivers and nurturers of life.

Circles of Influence

Just as God has designed women as lifegivers physically, He has also designed women as lifegivers spiritually. This is not to say that men are not called to share with others the life Jesus Christ offers, but that they do so *as men*, just as women share the truth of Christ *as women*, each uniquely fitted for the ministry of apologetics in specific ways.

Women care deeply about relationships. We can think of the relationships in which we exercise influence in terms of concentric circles, with the closest relationships, our family, filling our inner circle. As we move outward, the next circle may include extended family members, the next circle close friends, followed by acquaintances and perhaps co-workers in the next circle, with the largest outside circle comprising people whom we do not yet know, but may initiate relationships with for the sake of the gospel.

As we think about those in our circles of influence, we can identify those who are not believers and for whom we can intercede in prayer for salvation. As we do, we may learn of questions some of them have about Christianity. Even though we sometimes struggle with feelings of inadequacy when it comes to talking to others about spiritual things, God has designed us for this, so we can know that He will enable all that He asks of us.

Five Reasons We Can Know God Calls Women to Do Apologetics

God has commanded us as women not only to share that we believe in Jesus Christ but also the reasons why. Here are some evidences in Scripture that God has called women to think, study, and share the reasons for believing in Christianity:

1. We as women are created as **rational** beings who are called to love the Lord our God not only with our hearts, but also with our minds (Matt. 22:37). Our trust in Christ is grounded not in blind emotion, but in an intellectual appraisal of evidence that has convinced us of the truth of Christianity and given rise to a reasonable faith. Luke 10:38-42 records Christ's visit to the home of two women named Mary and Martha. When Martha complained that Mary was a slacker for not helping prepare the meal, Jesus praised Mary for listening to his teaching. Though He likely appreciated Martha's efforts in the kitchen, we can reasonably infer that He affirmed Mary's intellectual curiosity and commitment to a pursuit of truth.

As I have mentioned, one of the most troubling developments in women's ministry, in my opinion, is the focus on personal self-help and building self-esteem in women's conferences and discipleship groups. I am all for offering encouraging messages and building relationships, but women need more, and women can think. In fact, we as women must think and pursue intellectual development in order to love the Lord with our minds and to meet the needs spiritually of those we love, who ask difficult questions that may require some study on our part to answer clearly and accurately.

2. Women are **relational** beings who are called to love our neighbors as ourselves (Matt. 22:39). Our neighbors include people in our spheres of influence. In terms of our inner circle of immediate family members, our first spiritual responsibility, if we are married, is to our husbands. God urges us to love and respect our husbands (see Eph. 5). How can apologetics strengthen our marriage? If our husband is a believer, we can affirm the truths that build his faith as well as our own, and help him when he struggles with doubts.

What about those of us who are married to unbelieving husbands? When we learn the evidences for our faith, even if our husband is hostile to Christian claims, we can love him while not being shaken in our own faith. We won't use knowledge as a weapon against him. Instead, we are freed from defensiveness to practice 1 Peter 3:1-4, seeking to live out before our husband a life transformed by Christ so that he "may be won by [her] conduct." Former atheist and author of *The Case for Christ,* Lee Strobel, said his wife became a believer, and the change in the way she treated him and the children was so appealing that he embarked on his own search and eventually trusted Christ.

Another inner circle relationship in which apologetics can be helpful is with our children. Titus 2:5 (KJV) describes women as "keepers" at home who teach their children. "Keeping" implies watching over or guarding. Just as we fiercely protect our children physically, we must also fiercely seek their spiritual protection. Apologetics knowledge equips us to watch over and influence our children's worldviews.

Preparing ourselves will enable us to respond helpfully when our children are young and come home from playing with neighbor children, asking why their friends have shrines with little statues in their homes or why our family celebrates Christmas when the Jehovah's Witness friend does not. Later, we can dramatically impact the chances that our young adult child will grow in faith rather than walk away from Christianity disillusioned by living authentically and by being willing to learn and share foundational evidences that ground our faith.

Many resources are now available for teaching children how to rationally evaluate differing views in order to discern which is true, and also to develop and defend the Christian view of reality, the view that makes the most sense of the world around us. For example, apologist J. Warner Wallace has recently written a new apologetics book, a kids version of his wonderful book, *Cold Case Christianity*.

We can't expect our children to embrace the Christian version of reality and truth by just saying, "Because I said so." This response, like "You just need to have faith," isn't helpful, nor do these responses open dialogue or offer an accurate reflection of the substantial evidence for the truth our faith. But adding apologetics knowledge to our arsenal requires us to seek answers ourselves and not to shy away from our own hard questions and doubts.

Beyond our homes, our next circle of influence includes friends, and in particular, younger women, whom the Bible has mandated that we spiritually mentor. Titus 2:3-5 says,

> Older women likewise are to be reverent in behavior, not slanderers or slaves to much wine. They are to teach what is good, and so train the young women to love their husbands and children, to be self-controlled, pure, working at home, kind, and submissive to their own husbands, that the word of God may not be reviled.

As we learn the evidences supporting our faith, we can intentionally pass that knowledge on. Mentoring younger women in one-to-one relationships is vital to their growth and is an expression of our spiritual life-nurturing design. My mentor, Edna, and I taught a women's mentoring conference years ago, using our book *Woman to Woman: Preparing Yourself to Mentor*. Both younger and mature women were in the audience. We divided them into groups according to their seasons of life. Once the groups were separated, we asked the younger women why they didn't connect with the more mature women and asked the more mature women why they didn't connect more with the younger women.

When we reconvened the whole group, we shared what we had learned. It turns out that the younger women didn't think mature women wanted to be with them in their chaotic days and with their noisy kids. The mature women thought that the younger women didn't want to be with them because they were old, out of touch, and boring. More than a few tears were shed when they realized how much they needed each other. Mature women need younger women in their lives to energize them and help them stay connected with a community of friends.

Younger women need mature women in their lives to guide, counsel, and encourage them in the chaos that "this, too, shall pass." Developing mentoring relationships enables us to reach into another's life, and that's where the big questions come up in conversation as trust deepens.

In addition to mentoring younger women, our circles of influence include acquaintances and even people we don't yet know, including those of other faiths. Women are uniquely equipped to engage unbelieving women in faith conversations. For some groups of women, such as Muslim women, our willingness to engage them is their only hope for hearing about Christ in an understandable way, since they are prohibited from talking with men. With tension high between Muslims and other groups, sometimes they are lonely and just need a friend. We can be that friend.

3. We as women are **responsible** to bear witness of what we have seen and heard regarding Christ's identity and resurrection, and the numerous evidences for Christianity that God has instilled within the created order. According to Mark 16:1-11, women were the first witnesses of the empty tomb and were instructed to go tell others.

If Jesus entrusted women with the responsibility for speaking the truth about the single most pivotal event in human history, then we, too, can bear witness. And we can share not only our personal experience with Jesus Christ as the women at the tomb did, but also the historical, scientific, and philosophical evidences for the truth of Christianity that have been provided for us by our loving God. In so doing, we as women fulfill his command to make disciples of all nations (Matt. 28:19-20).

4. Another reason we can know that God has called women to do apologetics is that we as women are called to be **ready** to give cogent reasons for our beliefs, even if we must suffer to do so. 1 Peter 3:15-17, a banner scripture for apologetics, tells us:

> In your hearts honor Christ the Lord as holy, always being prepared to make a defense to anyone who asks you for a reason for the hope that is in you; yet do it with gentleness and respect, having a good conscience, so that, when you are slandered, those who revile your good behavior in Christ may be put to shame. For it is better to suffer for doing good, if that should be God's will, than for doing evil.

In the opening seven verses of 1 Peter 3, the apostle speaks first to husbands, and then to wives. Then, in verse 8, which culminates in the command of verses 15-17, Peter starts a new section, saying, "Finally, all of you," including both men and women in his subsequent appeal. This tells us that both men *and* women are called and honored to participate in Christ's suffering in defense of the faith.

5. Finally, we can know that God has called us to apologetics because the Scripture says that we as Christian women need to be **renewed** in the spirit of our minds (Eph. 4:11-24). We are not destined to ignorance about our faith and the rational evidences supporting our belief in Christ.

A friend once told me after reading *The DaVinci Code* that she wished she had never read it because it caused her to doubt. Such doubt can become debilitating when we fail to renew the spirit of our minds with truth, as we have talked about; we are tossed about with every new doctrine that arrives on the scene. Apologetics grounds our beliefs in strong evidence and makes our faith in Christ the most reasonable response to a God who has saturated the universe with witnesses to His presence and character.

So, when someone asks us why we think God wants women to do apologetics, we can share the five Rs. We can explain that God made women rational and relational beings, endowed us as responsible bearers of the truth, and provided us the knowledge with which to prepare ourselves and to renew our minds, so that we may be ready to share the overwhelming evidence that Christianity's claims are true.

One more observation is in order. Lest we get discouraged at the challenge facing us, we can rejoice at one positive effect of our culture's increasing hostility against Christianity. Here in America it is becoming more difficult to live as a nominal Christian—a Christian in name only—now that the name "Christian" is costing us. As we are mocked, rejected, and even viewed as evil, we are forced to batten down the hatches of our faith, making sure we really know Christ as Savior, and then cultivate the spiritual strength and knowledge to live counter-culturally for the cause of Christ.

As Christians, truth is on our side (or better said, we are on the side of truth). We can be energized by this fact. And we are not alone in our endeavor. We join the ranks of an emerging groundswell of thinking Christian women who are determined that the world will not have the last word in asserting that truth is relative, that God is an imaginary crutch for the weak-minded, that the Bible is a fairy tale, and that Jesus, if He lived at all, was just a good, moral teacher.

We choose to embrace our God-given identities as Christian women who are confident and ready to explain the reasons for the hope within. That's the purpose of this book. It's written for you, dear Christian friend, in whatever season of life you now find yourself, to equip you to stand strong and influence others toward Christ.

When we are willing to wholeheartedly pursue this knowledge, we will find that the evidence God has lavishly embedded in the artifacts of our world will lead us straight to the cross of Calvary on bended knee. We then can engage our loved ones, friends, and even strangers, by meeting them where they are, responding to their questions and objections, and walking them to the gospel.

3

Why Apologetics?

"I don't really think apologetics is of much use. You can't argue someone into faith," a friend commented when I told him about my field of study. This statement is, in fact, partially true. I can't argue someone into faith, but nor is that the purpose of apologetics. Of course, while we can't evangelize someone into faith, that doesn't stop us from sharing the gospel.

We use apologetics as pre-evangelism when people raise questions, to show that the Christian faith is well supported by evidence and thus, is reasonable. For those with doubts about the rationality of Christianity's claims, sharing evidences supporting its truth can be used by the Holy Spirit—the only one who brings someone to faith—to dismantle objections and open the heart's door to the gospel message.

We have talked about how we can know that God has specifically designed and called women to do apologetics. Now we will examine the broader rationale for using apologetics as a pre-evangelism tool. For those who do not think apologetics is biblical or useful, and there are Christians who do believe that, we can offer several logical and biblical reasons for including apologetics in our evangelistic toolbox.

1. Unbelievers ask sincere questions and deserve sincere answers.

Do you feel panic when a friend challenges your faith in Christ or asks a question you can't answer? Most of us can identify with that feeling. Though we don't need to worry about having the right answer for every question, it's also true that calmly and confidently responding to the challenges of unbelievers can bring glory to the Lord Jesus and open doors we thought were slammed shut.

I've heard for many years (and have told others) that when someone wants to debate, the best response is to share a personal testimony of what Christ has done in your own life, because no one can argue with that. I still do share my testimony, because the evidence of a changed life provides powerful proof that Christianity is true. At the same time, I also sometimes get the response, "Well, that's good if it works for you," with a quick change of subject. My testimony is important, but it cannot replace clear responses to sincere questions, and the truth is, not everyone asks questions just to argue. Some people really want to know the answers.

As we've discussed, some Christians believe that we should only share the gospel message, not detouring into philosophical issues and scientific evidences. I agree that we should share the truth from God's transforming Word (Hebrews 4:12). But, I have also met people who can't or won't accept the truth of Scripture because of nagging concerns they have about Truth, God, and Christianity. That's when I use apologetics. When I start by sharing the gospel, and then the person raises questions or objections about what I've said, I answer their questions and walk them back to the gospel.

Imagine a man is driving down a road and approaches a raised drawbridge that separates his country, where he lives under the control of a cruel dictator, and a neighboring country, where there is freedom. He longs to cross that bridge. Suppose you have the key to lower the drawbridge, but several miles before the bridge, numerous roadblocks have been set up. You could tell the driver all day how the key works to lower the bridge; however, that information won't help him until he can move past the roadblocks and actually get to the bridge. But, what if you knew how to dismantle each roadblock and explained this to him? Removing the roadblocks would open the way for him to reach the bridge, where he could use the key you've shared in order to lower the drawbridge, so he can cross to freedom.

Apologetic arguments remove the roadblocks that keep believers from being able to consider the claims of Christianity. As a pre-evangelistic tool, then, apologetics clears the way for the gospel message.

2. God Himself uses an apologetic approach to reach unbelievers.

Another reason for studying and sharing apologetics evidence for the truth of Christianity is that God Himself provides evidence to humans of His existence, power, and care for them. Given the fact that God is infinite, humans could only know God if He chose to make Himself known, that is, if He chose to reveal Himself. The evidence shows that God has indeed revealed Himself through **creation**. Evidence from the world around us that shows God exists, and reveals something about what He is like, is called **general revelation**. It leads us to **special revelation**, which is the gospel revealed in the Bible and in the person of Jesus Christ. General revelation shows us *that* God exists, and special revelation leads us to believe *in* Him through the work of Jesus Christ.

In Romans 1:18-21 Paul says about general revelation,

> What can be known about God is plain to them, because God has shown it to them. For his invisible attributes, namely, his eternal power and divine nature, have been clearly perceived, ever since the creation of the world, in the things that have been made. So they are without excuse.

This statement is consistent with other passages, such as Psalm 19:1, which says that the heavens declare the glory of God. Notice that these passages *in* the Bible cite evidences *outside* the Bible that show God exists.

Romans 2:15 explains that God has also implanted in humans a **conscience**. This conscience is a moral awareness of right and wrong, innate within man. The universal human awareness of right and wrong reveals the existence of a Supreme Moral Being: God. We'll talk more later about how the evidence of creation and the human conscience shows that a personal Creator God exists, but for now, we have confirmed that God Himself offers two evidences—creation and the human conscience—to prove He exists.

God in the flesh, Jesus, also used apologetics often. He offered as evidence of His deity, miracles, and He cited prophecies that He had fulfilled, so that people would believe in Him as Messiah. At the beginning of His public ministry He traveled to Nazareth, where He entered the synagogue on the Sabbath and read to listeners the prophecy of Isaiah, "The Spirit of the Lord is upon me, because he has anointed me to proclaim good news to the poor. He has sent me to proclaim liberty to the captives and recovering of sight to the blind, to set at liberty those who are oppressed, to proclaim the year of the Lord's favor" (Luke 4:18-19). Jesus then asserted that He Himself was the fulfillment of that prophecy. He spent the rest of His public ministry proclaiming that good news and providing physical evidence of His identity through healing and numerous other miracles.

When John the Baptist sat sequestered in prison, struggling with doubts, and sent word questioning whether Christ was the Messiah, Jesus didn't respond with, "You just need to have faith." Instead, He offered evidence: "Go and tell John what you hear and see: the blind receive their sight and the lame walk, lepers are cleansed and the deaf hear, and the dead are raised up, and the poor have good news preached to them (Matt. 11:2-6). After His resurrection, when His disciple, Thomas, rejected the witness of others that Jesus had risen from the dead, Jesus orchestrated an encounter that provided the evidence Thomas had requested, and seeing that evidence, Thomas worshiped the Lord (John 20:24-29). Through these examples, it is clear that God is willing and able to provide the evidence that will lead people to belief, when it is needed.

3. Early Christians and biblical writers used apologetics.

Scriptures record that New Testament believers provided evidence in order to break down barriers to the truth, to pave the way for sharing the gospel, or to clarify assertions that they made in their gospel presentations. Biblical writer Luke described an instance in which Paul used an apologetic approach in Acts 17:16-21. As you read the passage, identify action words showing that Paul used apologetics by offering rational arguments for the truth of Christianity's claims:

> Now while Paul was waiting for them at Athens, his spirit was provoked within him as he saw that the city was full of idols. So he reasoned in the synagogue with the Jews and the devout persons, and in the marketplace every day with those who happened to be there. Some of the Epicurean and

Stoic philosophers also conversed with him. And some said, 'What does this babbler wish to say?' Others said, 'He seems to be a preacher of foreign divinities'—because he was preaching Jesus and the resurrection. And they took him and brought him to the Areopagus, saying, 'May we know what this new teaching is that you are presenting? For you bring some strange things to our ears. We wish to know therefore what these things mean.' Now all the Athenians and the foreigners who lived there would spend their time in nothing except telling or hearing something new.

Paul reasoned with people in the synagogue and also in the marketplace. God-fearing Greeks and Jews worshipped in the synagogue, whereas the general Athenian population and Greek philosophers gathered in the marketplace. We know that Paul shared the gospel—evangelism—because he preached the good news about Jesus and His resurrection, offering them the opportunity to trust in Jesus.

That's just what we should do. If someone believes in the God of the Bible and trusts the Bible is true, we don't need to convince her of something she already believes. We can proceed directly to sharing the message of salvation through faith in Christ.

Notice, though, that some people "debated" (NIV) or "conversed" (ESV) with Paul in the marketplace. What evidence he shared in that setting, we aren't told. We do know that Jews in the synagogue already believed in the One True God, but they needed evidence that Christ was the Messiah that God had promised to send. The Athenians in the marketplace, on the other hand, worshipped a plethora of demonic idols as gods. Not only did they reject the notion of a Jewish Messiah, but also they rejected the idea of the One True God. This group had no respect for the Jewish Scriptures, so Paul could have shared scriptures until he was blue in the face, but they wouldn't have been impressed. Paul had to find common ground to open the door.

In addition to developing at least two different approaches in his presentation, Paul also had to keep in mind the thinking of two particular groups of philosophers, both of whom were way off the mark: the Epicureans and the Stoics. The Epicureans believed the goal of life was happiness obtained through human reasoning and that nothing beyond this life existed. The Stoics, on the other hand, believed that through their own goodness they could be god-like themselves, since reality, to them, *was* God. Paul had to offer rational reasons for believing in the

One True God by providing solid evidences for His existence that these people could understand and by dismantling intellectual objections so that they could believe in the one whom God sent. Let's see what happens next in Acts 17:22-29:

> So Paul, standing in the midst of the Areopagus, said: "Men of Athens, I perceive that in every way you are very religious. For as I passed along and observed the objects of your worship, I found also an altar with this inscription, 'To the unknown god.' What therefore you worship as unknown, this I proclaim to you. The God who made the world and everything in it, being Lord of heaven and earth, does not live in temples made by man, nor is he served by human hands, as though he needed anything, since he himself gives to all mankind life and breath and everything. And he made from one man every nation of mankind to live on all the face of the earth, having determined allotted periods and the boundaries of their dwelling place, that they should seek God, and perhaps feel their way toward him and find him. Yet he is actually not far from each one of us, for 'In him we live and move and have our being'; as even some of your own poets have said, 'For we are indeed his offspring.' Being then God's offspring, we ought not to think that the divine being is like gold or silver or stone, an image formed by the art and imagination of man."

Either by invitation or under duress, Paul was escorted to the Areopagus, a convocation of the city's well-respected council of elite thinkers. There he presented a systematic, rational argument—an apologetic—for the existence of a personal Creator God, beginning with a common point of reference, the Athenian altar to an unknown god. Arguing from history, he reasoned that he was not introducing a new god as some had accused. No, in their altar to the unknown god the Athenians themselves acknowledged the God that he was about to explain to them.

Paul's acknowledgment of the altar to an unknown god demonstrated that not only did he know the gospel, but he also knew the culture of the people he was trying to reach. Epimenides, a revered Cretan philosopher and poet, had evidently saved the city from a plague, hundreds of years prior, by proclaiming the existence of an unknown God and by building altars of worship to him.[2] Paul's knowledge of this cultural nuance is revealed in the fact that he referred in Titus 1:12-13 to a line from Epimenides' poetry. His cultural knowledge served him well in gaining a hearing, and we should follow his lead.

Paul then used a logical argument, saying that since the Athenians' own ancient writers had said, "We are his offspring," this God must have been the Creator of humans. Humans, then, whom God created, certainly could not create God by fashioning Him from metal or stone! Paul serves as a model for how to build bridges in diverse cultures so that the message of Christ may be heard and understood.

4. The Bible commands us to give well thought-out responses to questions about the Christian faith.

Several scriptures actually command or encourage us to use apologetics in defending the Christian faith. In 2 Corinthians 5:11, Paul said he tried to "persuade" unbelievers, which means to offer convincing evidence to change their minds. In Titus1:9-10, Paul urged Titus to select elders who would teach sound doctrine and who would "rebuke" or expose and correct errors of false teaching and teachers. In Jude 3-4, Jude urged believers to "contend" for the faith. The word "contend" in Greek is related to the word "agony." So, we are supposed to passionately defend the faith, whether correcting false teaching within the church or in the world among unbelievers.

The premier apologetic Scripture, 1 Peter 3:15, commands us always to "be prepared to make a defense to anyone who asks you for a reason for the hope that is in you; yet do it with gentleness and respect." The last phrase of this verse speaks about one aspect of apologetics often overlooked. We need to know not only what to say—the content—but also how to say it. Our tone should be gentle but firm. We show respect, not for the false belief, but for the person holding the belief, who, like us, is created in the image of God. Further, we learn to defend the faith without being defensive and to share an argument without being argumentative.

5. Believers need to strengthen their own faith.

During 10 years of teaching apologetics to high school students, I often told them that the confirmation of their faith was my first concern, not merely that they share with others. The summer after their graduation they would enter a university environment that was at best apathetic and at worst openly hostile to Christianity. While I wanted them to be able to articulate the evidences for the truth of Christianity to others, my primary burden was that student believers be confident in their own faith.

God has provided ample evidence to make us confident in our faith, and it is His desire that we mature in that faith, becoming more and more deeply convinced and able to articulate the overwhelming evidence of its truth. In Ephesians 4:11-24 (NKJV) Paul describes specifically God's plan for believers' maturing process:

> And He Himself gave some to be apostles, some prophets, some evangelists, and some pastors and teachers, for the equipping of the saints for the work of ministry, for the edifying of the body of Christ, till we all come to the unity of the faith and of the knowledge of the Son of God, to a perfect man, to the measure of the stature of the fullness of Christ; that we should no longer be children, tossed to and fro and carried about with every wind of doctrine, by the trickery of men, in the cunning craftiness of deceitful plotting, but, speaking the truth in love, may grow up in all things into Him who is the head—Christ—from whom the whole body, joined and knit together by what every joint supplies, according to the effective working by which every part does its share, causes growth of the body for the edifying of itself in love. But you have not so learned Christ, if indeed you have heard Him and have been taught by Him, as the truth is in Jesus: that you put off, concerning your former conduct, the old man which grows corrupt according to the deceitful lusts, and be renewed in the spirit of your mind, and that you put on the new man which was created according to God, in true righteousness and holiness.

How many Christians do you know who started out strong, only to end up compromising? Once faithful to a gospel-centered church, they now attend a church that preaches health and wealth as the right of every Christian. Or, perhaps someone you know was once committed to marriage but now embraces an immoral lifestyle that the Bible clearly calls sin. Or, what about the ones who were once leaders within the church but now settle for a tepid, nominal version of faith that costs them nothing but gains them friends? Such is the destiny of immaturity.

If we don't want this to happen to us, we need to listen to Paul, who in the above passage, explains not only the goal of the spiritual maturing process but also the means by which growth happens.

We join with the local church made of a body of believers over which God has placed leaders. The leaders prepare the saints for service through teaching, and the body of believers becomes built up and strengthened. The blessed result is unity in the faith and in the knowledge of Jesus. This means that individually we grow into "a perfect man," that is, a complete and mature believer, and as a church body we become fervent in living and sharing our faith. This maturity stabilizes our spiritual feet. We are no longer gullible children who are tossed around like ragdolls when the storms of false teachings and faddish doctrines blow our way.

So, we employ apologetics to respond to the questions and objections of unbelievers. We have strong biblical grounds for doing so, given the fact that God, Jesus Himself, and also biblical heroes of the faith, did so. Further, we do apologetics because scripture commands us to prepare ourselves to respond to false teaching and skeptical objections. Finally, we do apologetics because our own faith can be strengthened and matured.

4

What is Apologetics?

Though we often use the word "apology" to mean "saying you're sorry," the Greek word from which "apologetic" and "apology" come actually means to **give a systematic, rational defense**. Ancient philosophers, who debated their theories about truth, offered an "apologetic" for why their own philosophies made more sense than others. As a discipline, then, apologetics is a field of study that researches and offers rational evidence showing that Christianity's claims are true, and expresses those evidences in a coherent, systematic way. Evidence is drawn from a variety of sources from the natural world, such as from the disciplines of philosophy, logic, science, and history, as well as from the Bible itself.

We will discuss specific evidences derived from each of the above disciplines in more depth in the coming chapters, but here are a few examples. Philosophical and logical arguments are used to explain the evidence for truth being objective and absolute. Scientific evidences may be cited to show that the universe had a beginning and therefore requires a cause. Evidence from archaeology and history can be used to demonstrate the biblical writings are trustworthy.

The Content of Apologetics

There are several approaches to doing apologetics. In general, the approaches differ in their starting points. In this book I will use what is called the classical approach. The content of apologetics can be divided into three general topic sections.

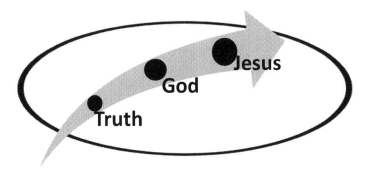

Truth

Assuming that the person with whom we are talking is a complete skeptic about the claims of theism and Christianity, meaning she doesn't believe in God (or has misunderstandings about what type of God exists), the traditional approach has been to start by sharing evidences for the theistic (personal Creator) God's existence, followed by offering evidence for the possibility of miracles, followed by presenting evidence for the reliability of the New Testament, and then finishing by explaining Jesus' claims and proof of being God, dying on the cross, and rising from the dead.

However, this approach has been modified over recent years due to the rise of postmodernist relativism. Now, when we as apologists attempt to offer as *true* the evidences for the existence of God, skeptics often respond by saying that there is no truth or that truth is relative. For this reason, apologists such as Norman Geisler have found it necessary to change the discussion starting point, logically backing up *from* first providing evidence for God's existence *to* first providing evidence for the existence of objective truth.

Once the existence of objective truth is established, then we can offer evidence for the truth claim that God exists. While some people think this move treats truth as existing before God, it does not. Rather, anxiety about discussing the existence of truth before discussing the existence of God arises from a category mistake. In the category of *being*, God is first. From Him flow all other existing things. But in the category of *knowing*, that is, how we obtain knowledge about reality, we must show that truth exists before we can offer evidence that it is *true* that God exists.

God

Once we have established the existence of objective truth, we discuss the evidence for God's existence. We may first clarify how various worldviews, such as pantheism, atheism, and theism, view God. A worldview is broader than a religion, and everyone has a worldview through which she interprets reality. Our worldview is best understood by how we answer questions about the origin, meaning, and destiny of the universe and of humans.

After distinguishing the main differences among worldviews, we can then share evidences for believing in the existence of the personal Creator God of theism. These lines of evidence include cause and effect (cosmological), order and design (teleological), and right and wrong (moral) arguments.

We may also talk about the reasonableness of believing a good, all-powerful God exists in light of the presence of evil in the world. In addition, we often address in this section issues related to the origin of life and humans, sharing evidence for the direct creation of humans and animals, rather than their emergence via naturalistic evolutionary mechanisms.

Showing that God exists and what kind of God exists logically precedes discussion about Jesus Christ, since we must first believe God exists in order to argue that Jesus Christ is God in the flesh. The discussion of God concludes by showing how, if the theistic God exists, miracles must be possible, and why science cannot rule out the possibility that miracles can occur. At this point, we are not yet trying to argue that the biblical miracles are true. That comes later, once we establish the reliability of the New Testament. What we want to show at this point is the evidence that miracles are possible, and that it is rational to believe that they can occur given the fact that God exists.

Jesus

The pinnacle of our apologetic is Jesus Christ. We open our discussion about Christ with evidence that the New Testament is trustworthy. We start here because the New Testament is our main source of information about what Jesus said and did in His ministry here on earth, and the New Testament verifies His identity as God.

We seek to show the reasonableness of believing that from the ancient manuscript copies on which our English translations are based, we can reconstruct with confidence what the originals said. Then we must show that the authors of those originals were the people who they claimed to be—apostles and their colleagues—who lived in the first century, and that they were people of integrity who spoke the truth. Our goal at this point is not to show that the New Testament is inspired by God and inerrant, but to show that when compared with other ancient historical documents, the New Testament meets (and exceeds) all the criteria for reliability that we would apply to other ancient documents.

Once New Testament reliability is confirmed, then we can talk about New Testament evidence of Jesus' claims to deity, as well as the claims of His deity made by others, including His friends, as well as some of His enemies. Once we have confirmed that Jesus did claim to be God and that His disciples also believed He was God, we can discuss evidence that He really was God. We explain His fulfillment of Old Testament prophecies, and evidence of His miracles, His perfection, His death, and His resurrection.

Once we have established His deity, then Jesus Himself, in His own words in the New Testament, confirms the truth and divine origin of the entire Old Testament. Also, the New Testament documentation of Jesus' words and actions reveals that while Jesus was on earth, He promised that the New Testament itself would be written, which we now have in our possession.

If the person with whom we have shared this wealth of evidence has responded to the Spirit's conviction and intellectual roadblocks have been removed, then she will be ready to receive the truth of the gospel. The gospel message should begin with an affirmation of God's creating humans to enter into relationship with Him, and humans' failure to attain God's standard of righteousness (Rom. 3:10, 3:23). Then we share that since we all have failed, we deserve death, i.e., separation from holy God, but we also share that God has offered us a gift of eternal life (Rom. 6:23). This gift of eternal life was provided to us, not after we became good enough to please God, but while we were still in sin rebelling against God. Christ stood in our place and took on the justified holy wrath of God against our personal sin (Rom. 5:8). We then explain that through trusting Jesus Christ as God in the flesh to forgive our sin, our relationship and peace with God can be restored (Rom. 10:13).

To arrive at this juncture in a conversation is a great joy. Nevertheless, no matter how far we get, we have shared truth. Sometimes we must be content, as apologist Greg Koukl says, with being a stone in someone's shoe, in getting her to think about these eternal issues and examine her own beliefs. But if we master the evidences for the truth of Christianity as well as learning the basic gospel message, we will be prepared to be used by the Holy Spirit however He sees fit.

Questions that Arise from the Three Topic Areas

We can divide the three broad topic areas of Truth, God and Jesus, into ten basic questions, questions we can learn to answer in conversations with family, friends, and co-workers. You will notice that the questions numbered 1-5 are answered with information external to the Bible, since we must first show evidence that truth exists, God exists, and that He has revealed Himself in the Bible, before arguing *from* the Bible that Jesus claimed and proved Himself to be God.

Truth

1) What is truth and does it exist?
2) How can truth be known?

God

3) Does God exist? If so, what kind of God?
4) How could God exist and evil be present in the world?
5) Is it rational to believe that miracles are possible?

Jesus

6) Why should we believe our copies of the New Testament are trustworthy?
7) Why should we believe what the New Testament writers wrote is true?
8) Did Jesus claim to be God in the New Testament?

9) What is the evidence that Jesus actually was God?
10) If Jesus is God, what does that mean for my life?

Where do we start a discussion if, say, someone already believes in the theistic God (#3) (such as a Muslim), but has other questions, such as #6-10, about the New Testament or Jesus Christ? We can start our conversation at the lowest numbered question (or topic in our three general categories: Truth, God, and Jesus) for which the questioner needs answers, and then move forward.

Sometimes we will even find that once we are discussing a topic, we may need to backtrack to a logically prior topic. That's fine. Conversations are seldom completely linear, and the purpose of lining up topics in logical order is so that we can deal with questions in a way that systematically moves toward the gospel message. But we don't need to get too rigid about the order. We just use the three topic categories and the questions #1-10 as a guide, so that if we get lost in a conversation, we can reorient ourselves to what logically comes next and know where to lead the discussion.

Also, be aware that it is not unusual for these conversations to take place over a period of time in which we are developing a relationship, rather than all in one sitting. We need to be willing to invest in the life of someone and take time to listen to her concerns. Our consistent love will speak louder than our words, at times.

5

Using Apologetics Wisely

It's important to discern in which situations apologetics knowledge is most helpful and ones in which other variables are at work so that a discussion of apologetics evidence may be counterproductive, or need to be postponed. This requires listening carefully to respond specifically to the needs of the unbeliever.

Let's start with an example. My friend Edna served as a camp counselor with her friend I'll call Megan, whom she learned during the week was not a Christian. Megan's problem with Christianity, though, had nothing to do with intellectual objections such as unanswered questions or misunderstandings about Christianity. One night the issue became clear when she said to Edna, "My mother loved me and she was a wonderful mother. But she didn't believe in Jesus. You can't tell me that my mother is in hell right now just because she wasn't a Christian."

Imagine if Edna had come at Megan with all the apologetics evidence that she could muster, proving that Christianity was true, and that indeed her mother was in hell. While Edna may have been right, she also would have hurt Megan so that she may never have turned to Jesus Christ.

The Thinker, the Feeler, and the Chooser

Years ago I listened to a series of audiocassettes by Bill and Anabel Gillham, called *Victorious Christian Living*,[3] in which Dr. Gillham, a Christian psychologist, described the three aspects of the human personality: the thinker, the feeler, and the chooser. The thinker is the intellectual aspect of our being. We reason, ponder, raise questions, analyze information, and come to conclusions in our understanding.

We also feel or experience emotions. When someone says something mean, we feel hurt. When our child makes the soccer team, we feel joy. When we hear a bump in the night, we feel fear. When a driver cuts in front of us, we feel angry. These are all aspects of our emotional being.

As humans we also have a chooser: our will. The will is the volitional aspect of our being. We choose what we will wear to work each day and what we will eat. We select from a wide variety of shoes on sale which three pairs we will buy. We choose a college, a spouse, and a place to live.

These three aspects of the human personality are interdependent, of course. We rarely choose to buy a pair of shoes we hate, for instance, and using our intellect, we may take hours thinking through the pros and cons of purchasing the spike-heeled, strappy red pair over the more serviceable but ugly loafers. But when an unbeliever expresses a negative response to Christianity, the barrier, or obstacle, generally expresses itself predominantly in one of the three areas, and apologetics is most helpful specifically for one of these areas.

The Type of Barrier Determines the Type of Response

Emotional Barriers

Megan faced an emotional barrier to belief. She struggled with fear and anger toward God when she realized that her mom, whom she dearly loved, was in hell. She saw God as unloving and resisted His invitation to trust Jesus Christ because she didn't want to be separated from her mom eternally. Anger toward God often characterizes an emotional barrier.

Fortunately, Edna immediately discerned the source of Megan's resistance to Christ and responded gently and lovingly. Instead of spouting apologetics evidence, she explained to Megan that whether her mom had chosen to trust Jesus or not, her mother loved her so much that she would want what was best for Megan, to trust Christ and know the blessing of His salvation.

We can share God's love with the one who is grieving or hurting, and offer the hope of forgiveness for the one who is weighed down with guilt. Though this person may also raise intellectual objections, she first needs to see that God loves her so much that He sent us to her side to care for her. We can share truth in the context of compassion. As time goes on, this person will want to deal with the questions underlying her emotional responses. And when that time comes, we will be prepared to answer.

Volitional Barriers

While Megan's barrier was emotional, some people simply don't want to submit themselves to the authority of Christ. I recall talking to a woman in her home about trusting Jesus. She listened attentively as I shared the plan of salvation, including appropriate scriptures. When I finished, I asked, "Would you like to accept Christ as Savior?" She looked me straight in the eye and quietly said, "No." When she gave no further explanation, I thought maybe I'd misunderstood and started over, reviewing the same information I'd just gone over. When done, I asked if she understood. She nodded. Once again I invited her to pray and ask Jesus to be her Savior. She simply said, "No."

Unbelievers may fully understand the essentials of the Christian faith, yet choose to reject it. Intellectually they may agree that the Bible is true from cover to cover. They may believe in a personal Creator God who sent His Son Jesus Christ to take the punishment for their sins. They may believe that Jesus Christ was born of a virgin, lived a sinless life, died on the cross, and rose again. The problem isn't unanswered questions or doubts (intellectual). It isn't that they are angry at God (emotional). They just don't want to submit to Jesus Christ's rightful authority over their lives. This is an issue of the will, not the intellect, and apologetics is not immediately helpful in these situations, though opportunities may arise at some point.

We can stay faithful to the Lord and stay close to the unbeliever. Many people who have come to faith after a long period of rebellion say that the most influential factor in their conversion was a friend who never gave up. Unless the friendship hurts our own faith or tempts us to compromise, we need to stay close and love this person. Interceding in prayer that God will soften her heart and showing how Christ has changed our own life can be powerful. Often, we will be able to share truth in small doses within the context of natural conversation.

Intellectual Barriers

Finally, some people have genuine questions and objections to the Christian faith. They may wonder how we can believe the Bible is true "when there are so many errors in it," or doubt that God can exist, given all the evil in the world. For these people, responding to their questions can dismantle barriers that are preventing them from seriously considering the truth claims of Christianity.

As a high school Bible teacher, one year I had a class of international students, most of whom were from China. The first year one student blatantly told me before class ever started that God did not exist. I explained to him that atheists could make an A in my class, and promised we would talk about the evidence, not just our convictions. I had planned to go slowly with these new students who had no context for understanding Christian truth claims, but the very first day of class he had me drawing responses all over the board to everything from his questions about multiple universe theory to the Trinity. I answered as best I could and prayed that God would open his heart. I also began chronological Bible storying to show that Christ preceded the history of the universe rather than coming late on the scene.

A pivotal moment occurred one day when we discussed evolution. He had only been taught Darwinian evolution as an explanation for the origin and development of the universe and all life, including humans. I showed a film on the fossil evidence found by researchers in China. When he realized that researchers from his own country disputed Darwinian gradualism by showing that new phyla (broad categories of body types) appeared fully formed during the Cambrian explosion, within a week he talked with a pastor and trusted Christ as Savior. Similar situations are ones in which apologetics is vital and effective. Sometimes people's hearts are ready to respond. Once their questions are answered they receive the gospel message with joy and trust Jesus. Even though some will never trust Christ, we will have been faithful to the Lord's call to share the truth.

Below I've listed a series of comments from unbelievers with different types of barriers to faith. See if you can identify the type of roadblock expressed in each comment: intellectual (thinker), emotional (feeler), or volitional—will (chooser).

1. "My brother was killed in a car accident three years ago. I don't see how a good God could let that happen to me, so I don't believe in God anymore."

2. "If I become a Christian, I'll have to quit living with my boyfriend. You can forget that."

3. "I don't think the Bible is true because in college my professor said they've found out that the New Testament wasn't even written by the real disciples. It was written hundreds of years later."

4. "I don't want to become a Christian right now. I don't need God. I'm doing pretty good on my own. Maybe when I'm old."

5. "It's okay if you need to believe in God. But what's true for you may not be true for me."

The individual in #1 has an emotional (feeler) barrier to faith. She feels angry with God, and we will want to start with listening and offering support, integrating evidence gently as questions arise. The unbelievers in #2 and #4 have volitional barriers; they simply don't want to choose to submit to Jesus Christ. The issues aren't intellectual objections or questions, so if we share evidence and the person rejects it, we will want to stay close, pray, be a true friend, and look for moments of openness. The individuals in #3 and #5 express intellectual barriers for which apologetics evidences will prove helpful.

How to Deal with the Person Who Just Wants to Argue

During the course of a conversation, sometimes people become argumentative, angry, and may verbally attack us. If they can keep us answering questions or tempt us to take a defensive tone, they can avoid addressing the real issues that keep them from responding in faith to Christ. People who don't listen to our answers, continually interrupt to criticize, or pepper us with questions without giving time to respond, may not be ready to receive the truth. These folks often raise intellectual objections to cover their volitional or emotional roadblocks, which hit close to home or cause them pain.

One of my seminary professors, Dr. Stephen Rummage, suggests that when someone becomes argumentative, that we calmly respond,

"You know, you are not the first person to ask this question. Theologians have been discussing this for hundreds of years." Second, we can ask, "If I answer all of your questions satisfactorily, will you then trust Christ?" Dr. Rummage has observed that most of the time they will respond, "No." For these folks, the problem isn't really an intellectual obstacle but an unwillingness to submit to God, even when truth is staring them in the face. At this point it may be time to close the conversation for now.

No matter what the barriers to faith are, we can remember the admonition of 1 Peter 3:15, which reminds us to answer everyone with gentleness and respect. I tell novice apologists that when we've done our best to please Jesus, He is honored even when we botch the argument. On the other hand, when we've crushed the opponent with wit and wisdom, we need to remember that there is no glory in winning the argument and losing the soul. If we present our arguments passionately yet tempered with grace, folks will remember the fragrance of Christ long after they have forgotten our words. They'll say, "I didn't agree with what she said, but she was gracious," and that in itself will soften their heart toward the Savior we proclaim and lend credence to our message.

Part 2

Talk About Truth

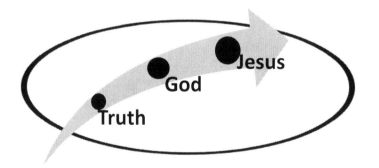

6

Truth on Trial

Truth has fallen on hard times in our culture in recent years. Ask most people under 30 to define truth and they will tell you it's whatever the individual makes it. Truth is relative according to most, meaning that truth is different for each individual. Closely related to this idea is the belief that truth is subjective, or is determined by our personal perceptions and feelings. "That may be true for you but not for me" has become the mantra of relativism. Lost on most people is the obvious implication of the relativistic view. If truth is individually "made up" and fluctuates based on personal feelings, then by definition, it is not truth. Every person defining what is true for herself results in there being no such thing as truth. We are left with mere opinion.

Many people argue that they don't believe in Christianity because we think we are right and everyone else is wrong. Interestingly, the same people who assert this also believe that they are right and Christians are wrong. Christianity is not the only religion that makes truth claims. Every religion/belief system makes truth claims that can be evaluated as true or false based on the evidence.

Hinduism, a pantheistic worldview, claims that God is the universe. All existing things are god and therefore, everything in the universe, down to a blade of grass, is in some sense divine. Atheism claims there is no God. All that exists in the universe and the universe itself came into being on its own, from nothing, and by nothing. All of nature is all there is. Theism claims there is only one God, and that God is a personal Creator, not a mere force. If the pantheistic view is right about the nature of God, then atheism and theism cannot be true. And if Christianity is right about God, then atheism and pantheism are false. If atheism is right that there is no God, then pantheism and theism are false. So, when someone says, "You Christians are narrow-minded. You think your beliefs are the only ones that are right," you can say, "And you think that you are right and I am wrong. We both think that our beliefs are true and that opposite beliefs are false. That is not due to being narrow minded; it is the nature of truth."

Christianity, a theistic worldview, claims that it is true that Jesus Christ is God, died for our sins, and physically rose from the dead. When we claim something is true, we make a claim about reality: the real world. Different philosophic views vary as to whether they believe objective reality, the real world, actually exists. Some believe reality is only a product of imagination (of course, they have trouble proving that).

Views About the Nature of Truth

In John 18:38 Pilate asked Jesus the question, "What is truth?" Even though he may have posed his question sarcastically, the question itself reflects one of man's most fundamental concerns. Truth may be defined as what matches reality. So, a truth claim is an assertion that someone believes expresses the truth about reality. If I say that today is Tuesday, it is either Tuesday or it is not, as relates to this specific location in the world. Whether my claim is true or not is determined by whether it is indeed Tuesday: whether it matches the way things really are.

Not all sentences are truth statements. Statements or propositions are the kinds of sentences that assert something as true or false about reality. For example, "I don't like beets," expresses an opinion, not a proposition. It is a subjective comment about your preference. "Those vegetables in that cooking pot are beets," is a proposition. They are either beets or they are not, and the truth or falsity of the statement may be assessed according to whether the statement accurately reflects or corresponds to reality. This is called the correspondence view of truth.

The correspondence view of truth is only one among several views in our Western culture, but certainly is the one that we live out in daily life. Some argue for the coherence view of truth. Truth is what is internally consistent. But just because a group of suspects conspires to contrive an internally consistent timeline of events to exonerate themselves does not mean the timeline is true. It is possible that a more complex, messier timeline is true instead.[4]

Still others argue that the pragmatic view of truth is the most accurate view of reality. Whatever brings about the desired goal is what is true. But we all know people who accomplish goals in deceptive, untruthful ways.

A look at several passages of scripture will demonstrate how it is the correspondence view of truth that is revealed in the Bible. In Acts 5:1-11 the story Ananias and Sapphira demonstrates that God took very seriously their false claims, because their claims didn't match reality. Both Ananias and Sapphira claimed that that they had brought to the apostles the full amount of their profit from a land sale. The apostles confirmed that they had both lied to God, and Ananias and Sapphira lost their lives because of their deception. Their claim didn't correspond to the way things actually were, and they were held accountable in a dramatic way.

In Genesis 3 the narrative recounts the fall of Adam and Eve into sin. Satan promised that they would not die if they disobeyed God by eating the fruit of the forbidden tree. But Satan lied. Death in Scripture refers to separation. Physical death refers to separation of the material body from the immaterial soul/spirit of man, and spiritual death refers to separation of the person from God. From the moment that Eve ate of the tree, she learned that God's promises are true, for immediately she was spiritually separated from God, and her body began to deteriorate, culminating in physical death. God's corresponded to reality; Satan's didn't.

In Exodus 20 the Ten Commandments forbid giving false testimony about another person. False testimony refers to asserting something that is at odds with reality. Finally, in the book of 1 John 21:24 the apostle speaks of himself in third person, describing an interaction between Peter and Jesus. John says after describing the facts of the events, "This is the disciple who is bearing witness about these things, and who has written these things, and we know that his testimony is true." Each of the preceding passages defines truth, not as that which is pragmatic, coherent, or a matter of perception, but as that which corresponds to reality.

Is Truth Merely What I Make It?

In his book *Reality Isn't What It Used to Be*, Walter Truett Anderson says,

Constructivists—whose thinking runs close to my own . . .—say we do not have a "God's eye" view of nonhuman reality, never have had, never will have. They say we live in a symbolic world, a social reality that many people construct together and yet experience as the objective "real world." And they also tell us the earth is not a single symbolic world, but rather a vast universe of "multiple realities."[5]

In the constructivist view we do not experience reality; we make it. And every person's reality is different. Now, he is not saying that we each *perceive* reality differently. We certainly do. He is saying that there is no reality "out there," only "in here," generated by our own thoughts.

Contrast this view with that of Christianity, which proposes that truth is not relative but absolute, not subjectively constructed, but objectively existing. As absolutists we believe that a statement that is true, is true *for* all people. And as objectivists we believe that reality is not merely something constructed by the mind, but that the truth claims are made about real things in a real world that exists external to our minds. Also, notice that in the objectivist view of reality the determiner of what is true is the *object* in reality (thus, objective), not the *subject* perceiving the object (thus, subjective). Let's look at an example.

When I claim the traffic light is red at this moment in time, the truth of that assertion is determined, not by my personal perception, but by the status of the traffic light itself. This does not mean I can always *know* what the color of the light is. I may have a defect that distorts my perception of color. That is a different issue. Nevertheless, whether the light is green or red is not a property of my perception, but of the object.

I often hear people counter that for the person whose visual impairment causes her to see the red light as green, it is actually *true for her* that the light is green. This is an understandable confusion, so we need to clarify what we mean when we say that something is true for everyone. We simply mean that whatever assertion is made about the object in question is not changed by any individual's *perception*, but is determined by the status of the object itself. Think about it this way. If the woman caused an accident due to her misperception that the traffic light was green instead of red, she would still be ticketed by the police officer. Her perception did not alter reality—the way things actually were. The light was, in fact, red, despite her personal perception of it being green.

The same principle applies to assertions related to places. It may be freezing cold in Greenland and burning hot in the Sahara. However, this does not show truth is relative to place. It is true for people in all places that it is freezing cold in Greenland (if it is) and also burning hot in the Sahara (if that is the case). We must properly identify and keep in view the object, or referent, about which we are speaking, in order to make truth claims about it.

We will also come across people who argue that truth changes over time and therefore, is relative to time. Their arguments may go something like, "We didn't used to believe in gravity; now we do. So truth changes over time."

These kinds of comments demonstrate the ingrained desire of humans to be the boss of themselves and not submit to the reality of objective truth. Our knowledge and beliefs change over time, but the truth does not change. If gravity is a property of our earth since the inception of time, space, and matter, then whether we came to believe it existed or not does not change the reality of its existence. It is true for all time that gravity existed. What about events that are limited to certain segments of time, such as who is president? It will be true for all time that J.F. Kennedy was president of the United States from 1961-1963.

Consequences of Relativism

I asked a Hindu woman one day (we will call her Aashi) if two opposite statements could both be true. She responded, "Of course." Let's apply that claim to an example. If I claim that a personal Creator God exists, then the opposite of that statement—a personal Creator God does not exist—can *also* be true, in exactly the same sense. But even the Hindu woman does not practice her professed belief in her daily life.

Aashi actually believes that if her friend Tamanna says she just picked up Aashi's veggie burger from the drive thru and it is in the bag, that when Aashi looks in the bag, the veggie burger will actually be there. But when Aashi looks in the bag, it isn't there and she says so. As a relativist she has a problem. Tamanna says it's in the bag and Aashi says it isn't. Aashi has no choice but to accept the possibility that the burger could both be in the bag and not in the bag at the same time. The upshot of all this is that we all know, including Aashi the relativist, that the veggie burger can't be both in the bag and not in the bag at the same time.

Let's play out the consequences of relativistic thinking a bit more. If relativism is true, then we could not convict someone for murdering, since it could be true also for the murderer that killing was not actually murder because the victim stepped on her toe when walking by and deserved it. (Some people may believe this, but they will find themselves in jail.)

If relativism is true, a statement could be true and false at the same time and in the same sense. The time could be 3:00 p.m. at a certain location, and at the same time and in the same exact sense *not* be 3:00 p.m.

If relativism is true, no one would ever be wrong about anything. (I only like that option when it works my way.) If you say 3 + 3 equals 6 and I say that 3 + 3 equals 24, we could both be right. So much for mathematics.

Lastly, a person who believes "Truth is relative to each person" actually believes that this principle is true universally *for every person*. If she believes that her statement is true for everyone, then she really believes that truth is objective and absolute (that this is a truth about reality external to the mind and is the same universally for all people). She's not a very good relativist, after all.

One final example. Imagine a relativist going to the bank to withdraw $200. She speaks to the teller who says there is not $200 in the account, only $100. The relativist explains to the teller that she knows there is $200 in her account because she just deposited $5000 two days ago, has made no withdrawals, and has the receipt verifying her balance. Not even the relativist would accept a teller responding, "Well, that may be true for you, but it is not true for me. You can't have the money." Yet this is exactly what relativists must live with in order to practice relativism in their daily lives.

7

How We Know Things

If reality exists, the question still remains as to whether it can be known. Agnostics say we cannot (or do not) know reality. Yet, when making that claim, they are claiming that they know *that* truth about reality.

Skeptics argue that it is most reasonable to doubt everything. Of course, they don't doubt that they should doubt everything. They're absolutely certain of their conviction.

Realists such as Christians assert that by its nature, reality is knowable. To say reality is knowable simply means that things in reality have distinguishable natures. We can't help but interface with these things because they press upon our senses. To say that reality is not knowable is self-defeating, in that when making that claim, the person is claiming to know something about reality, namely, that it is not knowable.

Although reality by nature is knowable, this does not mean that *humans* can know everything they would like to know about reality. When we say humans can know truth about reality we are referring to our human *ability* to access things in reality and appraise them through our senses and intellect. As finite creatures we have limitations in our ability to access and appraise the properties of things in the universe, and our judgments may even sometimes err. But the only way we could ever know we made a mistake in our judgments about reality is if we could really know reality. If we could not know reality, we would never know we made a mistake in our judgment about it.

We can know truths about things in reality according to various levels of certainty. Some truths are undeniable, as we will show. Other truths may be known according to levels of probability.

How We Think: Laws of Logic

Universal principles of thought, also called *first principles* or *laws of logic*, provide the foundation for all human thinking. They are called first principles specifically because they do not have to be proven; they are self-evident. In fact, any effort to deny them actually demonstrates their truth. We will give an example in a moment.

These laws are not laws we make, like ought-to kinds of laws that assert moral obligations. They are laws that we discover. They are inherent in reality and govern the way we as humans think and communicate.

There are three main laws of logic, and when we first read them, we may be tempted to say, duh! That's because we take these laws for granted. But knowing about these laws is useful, because people who believe in relativism—that truth is different for every person—deny these laws. So, when we say that the Bible is true, they may say, "Well, that may be true for you but not for me." Their comment suggests that the Bible could be both true and not true at the same time. The laws of logic show this cannot be possible.

Understanding these laws can help us to respond to relativistic claims by showing that objective truth does exist. Once we've agreed on truth's existence, then we can move forward in our conversation and argue such points as, "It is true that the theistic God exists," and "It is true that the New Testament is trustworthy." We can then evaluate these claims in terms of the evidence. If we don't first establish that truth exists, then when we make our other assertions, we may get sidetracked into a discussion of whether any of these claims can just be true for me while not for another person who has a different, but just as valid, truth.

1. The Law of Identity: A is A.

"A banana is a banana."

The law of identity says that a thing is that thing. A thing has a nature, an essence or "stuff-ness" that makes the thing what it is. The thing's essential characteristics distinguish it from other things in the world. This is how we know that a banana is not an apple.

2. The Law of Excluded Middle: Either A or not A.

Either, "It's a banana," is true, *or* "It's not a banana," is true. There is no middle option.

This is an "either—or" statement. Notice that we are not saying that the thing is either a banana or it is an apple. The assertion is much more foundational and self-evident. It is either a banana or it is not a banana. There is no middle possibility between those two options. Now, we could say that a pluot is a hybrid of an apricot and a plum, but it is either a pluot (a hybrid between a plum and an apricot) or it is not a pluot. Remember, when evaluating truth claims, we must keep the object we are talking about in view.

3. The Law of Non-contradiction: A is not non-A.

"It can't be both a banana and NOT a banana at the same time and in the same sense."

Particularly useful for our apologetic purposes, the Law of Non-contradiction says that two opposites cannot both be true at the same time and in the same sense. Another way of stating this law is that something cannot be both true and false at the same time. So, it cannot be true that Christ is God and that Christ is not God at the same time. Also, by way of application, if the Christian view that Christ is God is true, then the Muslim view that Christ is not God cannot also be true.

As an everyday example, your car cannot both be in your driveway and not in your driveway at the same time and in the same sense. Now, it could be in the driveway in the sense that the front is in the driveway and, in a *different* sense, it may not be in your driveway, because the back of the car is protruding into the road (possible, though not smart).

Persons who deny the existence of these laws, such as the Law of Non-contradiction, actually *use them* to make that claim. Let me explain. Recall the Hindu woman who asserted that two opposite statements could both be true, which means she denies the Law of Non-contradiction. Let's look at the implication of her statement in light of the Law of Non-contradiction. Below, her assertion and the opposite assertion are written:

Hindu woman: "Two opposite statements *can* both be true."
Tricia: "Two opposite statements *cannot* both be true."

If she is right, (two opposite statements can both be true) then it is actually possible for *both* of the opposite statements above to be true. Unfortunately for her, she has defeated her own statement!

She actually employed the Law of Non-contradiction in making her own assertion, because in making her statement, by implication she assumes that my statement is false, which is exactly what the Law of Non-contradiction says. She cannot escape the implications of the Law of Non-contradiction no matter how hard she tries.

Through these foundational laws of logic God communicates with us and we communicate with each other. They are true across time and culture. Laws of logic enable us to know that opposites can't both be true and something is either that thing or it is not that thing.

Other Ways of Knowing: Deductive and Inductive Reasoning

While the laws of logic can tell us that a statement in the argument below can be true or false, but not both at the same time, they cannot tell whether any of the statements actually *is* true or if the conclusion (#3) logically follows the premises (#1 and 2). We use deductive and inductive reasoning to figure that out. Read the deductive argument below:

1. All women are athletic.
2. Jane is a woman.
3. Therefore, Jane is athletic.

When we share an apologetic *argument* supporting a truth claim of Christianity, we are not referring to a heated debate. Rather, an argument is a group of assertions in which we claim that a conclusion logically follows the premises. The premises in an argument are reasons offered for accepting the conclusion. As we read through an argument, we draw inferences about the logical relationships between the statements.[6]

A deductive argument is one in which the premises and conclusion are related in such a way that if the premises are true, then the conclusion must be true. As we converse with people, we can practice identifying the premises and the conclusion of an argument, even when they are not formally stated. In terms of apologetic arguments, examples of deductive arguments that we use are the cause and effect, order and design, and right and wrong arguments for the existence of God.

In the argument above, *if* it is true that Jane is a woman, and *if* it is true that all women are athletic, we can know for sure (necessarily or 100%) that Jane is athletic. Of course, this argument's conclusion is false, even though the argument is valid, because one of the premises is not true.

In order to find out if the premises (#1 and #2) are true, we use another method of attaining knowledge called inductive reasoning (also called the scientific method). In an inductive argument, we appraise things in the world by our senses (seeing, hearing, touching, smelling), and intellectually generalize principles about the world based upon our observations. When we gain knowledge this way, the limitation is that we cannot know with 100% certitude that our conclusions are true. We may have evaluated 20 million women and found them all to be athletic, but perhaps there are some we have not evaluated who are couch potatoes.

As applied to apologetics, we could develop an inductive argument for the second premise in the cause and effect argument for God's existence. The second premise says, "The universe had a beginning." We can present several scientific evidences that affirm that the universe is not eternal. Then, we can conclude that it is reasonable to believe that the universe did have a beginning.

There are a few things that are known with 100% certainty. We can know that we exist, since we must exist in order to say we don't exist. We can know mathematical principles such as $2 + 2 = 4$. But for most things, we know them according to varying levels of probability. In our legal system, we consider something to be true if the evidence supports the truth claim *beyond a reasonable doubt*. In fact, in most of life we are quite content and successful by applying the principle of reasonable doubt to evaluating truth claims. This principle will serve us well in evaluating evidences for the truth of Christianity, as well as in navigating successfully throughout life in general.

In evaluating the claim that God exists, the foundational laws of logic enable us to know that God cannot both exist and not exist. Then, we use inductive reasoning to determine whether the evidence supports the truth of the premises beyond a reasonable doubt. We also apply deductive reasoning to see if our conclusion follows logically from the premises, making the argument valid. If it does, and our premises are true, then we can know that our conclusion is true.

An example of a deductive argument that we use to demonstrate that the design of the universe requires an intelligent being goes like this:

1. Everything that exhibits specified complexity is caused by an intelligent being.
2. All living things demonstrate specified complexity.
3. Therefore, all living things are caused by an intelligent being.

This is laid out as a deductive argument. So, if it is true that everything demonstrating specified complexity is caused by an intelligent being rather than by natural, random causes, *and* if it is true that all living things demonstrate specified complexity, then it is necessarily (100%) true that all living things are caused by an intelligent being.

Our challenge, first, is to define what we mean by specified complexity and an intelligent being. Once we have defined our terms, we then assess through our senses and intellect the evidence supporting our premises. For example, for premise #2, we can sample a large portion of living things in our world, and even though we cannot prove with 100% certainty (maybe we missed an organism somewhere that is specifically complex but not caused by an intelligent being), we can logically conclude beyond a reasonable doubt that all living things demonstrate specified complexity. (As an aside, we can argue that once the natures of things are identified according to their essential properties, we can generalize to larger populations also. But this is a different discussion.)

At any rate, we are using inductive reasoning, which involves assessing specific examples and then generalizing to a larger population. We seek to show beyond a reasonable doubt that the premise for which we are providing evidence, is true.

8

The Boomerang Effect

When I was in Australia years ago, my family and I took lessons on how to throw a boomerang. Boomerangs are fascinating instruments. Hurl one into the air and it comes back to you. There is one danger. If you're not careful, you might get whacked in the head by your own boomerang. People who believe truth is relative often make self-defeating claims about truth that boomerang on them. In fact, apologist Norman Geisler asserts that virtually all non-Christian worldviews espouse self-defeating assertions.[7]

Geisler defines a self-defeating claim as one that doesn't meet the standard set forth in the claim itself. Formally known as the "principle of self-falsification," says Geisler, the principle is not self-evident as are laws of logic, but it *is* based on the Law of Non-contradiction. A statement is self-defeating, or self-refuting, "when it entails two statements that are contradictory, one that it makes explicitly and a contradictory one implied in the very act or process of making the first one."[8]

So, for example, when someone says, "I cannot speak a word of English," we recognize immediately that the person has contradicted herself. She has not met her own standard—not speaking a word of English—since she is speaking in English to make the claim. The explicit statement is, "I cannot speak a word of English." The implicit statement embedded in the claim is, "I am speaking this statement in English."

To help a person understand the self-defeating nature of her claim, we might respond, "But aren't you saying that in English?" When we make such a comment, we demonstrate that the claim logically boomerangs on itself. (Norman Geisler and Frank Turek call this the *Road Runner Tactic* and Greg Koukl calls it the *Suicide Tactic*.)

Christian philosopher J.P. Moreland identifies three characteristics of a self-defeating statement:

1. It establishes some requirement of acceptability for an assertion (or sentence, proposition, or theory).
2. It places itself in subjection to this requirement.
3. It fails to satisfy the requirement of acceptability that the assertion itself stipulates.[9]

The usefulness in identifying self-defeating statements cannot be overstated. Once an assertion is identified as self-defeating, no further argument can be offered that is based upon that belief. As we learn to recognize self-defeating statements, we will notice people making these kinds of statements frequently. We may even find them in our own reasoning patterns.

We can help people recognize their errors in thinking when we point out the self-defeating nature of the claims. Our goal is not to humiliate, but to show the logical inconsistency of the claim. We will talk more about how to say things in an edifying and redemptive way later in the book. Our ultimate hope is that the individual will give more thought to her view and reconsider the claims of Christianity.

Let's examine the following statements and determine which ones are self-defeating, what makes them self-defeating, and how we can respond.

1. "Science is our only source of truth."

This is a common assertion by those who hold science in high regard. Atheist chemist Peter Atkins says, "Science can deal with all the serious questions that have troubled mankind for millennia. My view is that **science is without bound**" [boldface in original].[10]

If science is our only source of truth, then that very statement cannot be true. It is a philosophical assertion, or opinion, not a scientific statement. To bring the self-defeating nature of the comment to someone's attention we might respond by saying that if science is our only source of truth, then we cannot include this statement as one of those truths, since the statement itself cannot be evaluated by any scientific method using our senses.

Possible responses include:

"If science is our only source of truth, then your statement, which is not scientific, cannot be true."
"Is that a scientific statement?"
"How has that statement been scientifically tested?"
"Since your statement is philosophical, not scientific, how can it be true?"

2. "Only statements written in English are true."

We do not have enough information to say whether this statement is true or not. Now, intuitively, we know it is false, and we can confirm it is false by investigation. But, remember, a false statement is not always a self-defeating statement.

3. "Only propositions verifiable by the senses are true."

Skeptic philosopher David Hume said something similar to this assertion. Of course, he did not admit to it being self-defeating. If only propositions verifiable by the senses are true, then this proposition, since it is an abstract thought and not verifiable by the senses, cannot be true. Don't get hooked by the fact that the statement is written, so we can verify the writing with our eyes. The assertion itself is an abstract concept that is purely philosophical and cannot be verified by the senses. Therefore, it is self-defeating.

An interaction about this self-defeating statement could look something like the following:

Christian: "That proposition is not verifiable by the senses, and by your definition, cannot be true."

Unbeliever: "Well, you can read this proposition, so it can be verified by the senses."

Christian: "The writing can be verified by sight, but the proposition itself is an abstract concept, and therefore, is not verifiable by the senses."

4. "I do not exist."

The speaker must exist in order to make the assertion, so the assertion is clearly self-defeating. When someone insists she does not exist, Norman Geisler sometimes responds by inviting her to jump off a building. Of course, he is being facetious. He is driving home the point that if she really believed she didn't exist, then she wouldn't have a problem jumping off a building, since she wasn't really there to experience the fall. The truth is, she really believes that she exists, since no normal person would jump off a building just to prove her point.

Other possible responses may include:

"I don't hear anyone speaking" (since no one exists).

"You expect me to believe *you* and yet you say *you* don't exist."

5. "God does not exist."

Unless God were speaking this sentence, it would not be self-defeating. We must look at the evidence before knowing whether this assertion is true. So, it is not self-defeating, even though it may be false. When we study the arguments for God's existence, we will look at the evidences that we can appraise in order to support our assertion that God exists.

6. "We cannot know truth."

It is interesting that people who assert this believe it is *true* that we cannot know truth! If we cannot know truth, then how could we possibly know whether that statement was true? This statement is, therefore, clearly self-defeating.

"If we cannot know truth, how do you know that statement is true?

"Is *that* statement true?"

7. "Language has no meaning but what the reader gives it."

This comment is very common in university English departments. The view that there is no inherent meaning in text itself has also infiltrated evangelical biblical studies. Norman Geisler affirms that more and more evangelical authors "are surrendering to the postmodern influence of relativism in interpretation."[11] To deny that the text has inherent meaning is to deny objectivity of meaning and to affirm that meaning is subjective, i.e., up to the interpretation of the individual reader, and therefore, relative to person.

Professor of biblical studies, Thomas Howe, explains the significance of the claim that language has no meaning: "With the rejection of objective meaning comes a rejection of objective truth."[12] If truth is a quality of statements and those statements must be interpreted., then truth is up to the individual interpreter, and thus, no objective truth exists.

The fact that the claim is self-defeating produces little angst for most postmodern subjectivists. But if it is true that "language has no meaning but what the reader gives it," then I, the reader, may legitimately argue that this assertion itself actually means that gooseberries in winter grow into mushrooms in summer. The problem in this instance is that the person making the statement expects me as the reader to understand *exactly* what she means by *her* assertion, rather than supplying my own meaning to it. Again, in this case, this particular statement is self-defeating.

Possible responses include:

"Do you expect me to understand *your* statement, or do I give *your* statement meaning?"

"I'm sorry; I can't understand your language in that statement."

We need to be prudent in our identification of self-defeating claims. As we have observed, sometimes a claim is false but not self-defeating. "The earth is standing still," is a false claim, but it is not self-defeating. We could say that all self-defeating claims are false, but not all false claims are self-defeating. As Moreland says, we must make sure "that the statement actually refers to itself, that it is part of its own subject matter."[13]

Here's one example of a statement that is false but not self-defeating, even though we may be tempted to label it as such: "There are no moral absolutes." At first glance, it may look like a self-defeating statement. It is false, but it is not self-defeating. Moreland explains, "The statement is a philosophical assertion about morality and not a claim of morality. To be a claim of morality, an assertion must be a moral rule such as 'Do not kill,' and this statement is not such a moral rule."[14] When Moreland says that it is not a claim *of* morality he means that while the claim makes a statement about morality, the claim in itself is not a moral claim. It is a false claim, and we could demonstrate this through good reasoning. But it is not a self-defeating claim.

As we have also seen, sometimes we cannot know whether a claim is false until we gather more evidence. A person who says, "I can't speak a word of French," is not making a self-defeating claim. It may be true or false that she cannot speak a word of French. We need more information to know. However, if the person made this statement in French, then it would be self-defeating.

Start listening carefully to how people speak, and monitor your own assertions in order to identify self-defeating statements that you may make. Choose wisely when to respond to self-defeating assertions in a way that will help the person see the error in her line of thinking. Even if you don't respond to an individual by pointing out the self-defeating nature of such a claim, the very fact that you recognize self-defeating claims can be a helpful tool in strengthening your personal faith.

Finally, even when we point out the self-defeating nature of a statement, we shouldn't be surprised if the person gets angry and accuses us of nitpicking or trying to trick her. In other cases, the skeptic completely ignores the observation and moves on. Logically speaking, no further argument can be built on a self-defeating statement. But this does not stop many people in our relativistic society. Some are quite comfortable with the contradictory nature of their assertions. Nevertheless, because the argument of many skeptics against Christians is that our faith is illogical, we can point out to them that, at least in this case, it is not the Christian who is making an illogical claim, but the one making the self-defeating claim.

Part 3

Talk About God

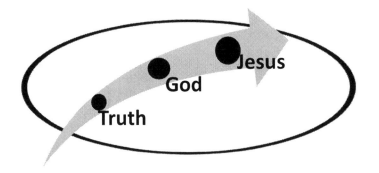

9

How You See It: What's a Worldview?

Every person interprets reality based on her overarching mental picture of reality called a worldview. A person's worldview can be identified by how she answers the big questions of life about the universe's and humans' origin, the nature of humans, whether and how reality can be known, the meaning of human life, the nature and origin of morality, and the ultimate destiny of humans. Knowing a person's worldview can guide us in directing the conversation to relevant issues. For example, if the person believes that humans originated through evolution and that after death our destiny is for our bodies simply to rot in the ground with no afterlife, then we can direct the conversation toward evidence for the existence of God.

There are three main worldviews: atheism, pantheism, and theism. They are differentiated specifically by their beliefs about God, as well as by beliefs about other aspects of reality.

Atheism is the view that no God exists. Contemporary atheists often verbalize this view as a "lack of belief" in God, or as a belief in "one less God" than theists. While many atheists argue that their view does not constitute a religion, they do believe certain things about ultimate reality. For example, they often assert that humans gradually evolved from lower forms of life, through naturalistic processes. Humanism and some forms of Buddhism are atheistic.

Pantheism asserts that God *is* the universe and all that is in it. The grass, buildings, and humans are all aspects of God. Humans are to God as drops of water are to the ocean. This is why Hindus, whose religion is pantheistic, say, "Namaste," as a greeting. Though some Hindus say that it is merely an innocuous greeting without meaning, others affirm that it means, "I bow to the divinity within you." They believe that humans are divine, but have forgotten, and need enlightenment in order to remember their true divine identity.

Theism is the belief in a personal, Creator God who is beyond the universe (transcendent), but is also active in the universe (immanent). Theists also believe that God is all-knowing, all-powerful, and perfectly holy and good. The three main theistic religions are Orthodox Christianity, Orthodox Judaism, and Orthodox Islam. I say "orthodox" to refer to the historical form of the religion.

Each of these religions exhibits newer derivative forms, or has spawned completely new religions. For instance, Judaism is traditionally monotheistic, believing that only one God exists, and that He is revealed in the Torah (in general, the Old Testament, or more specifically, the first five books). Some newer branches of Judaism, however, do not believe that the Old Testament is divinely authored. Thus, they do not maintain a scriptural view of God.

Islam has many branches, most prominent of which are Shia and Sunni forms. Moreover, in many African countries where Islam is practiced, it is blended with African traditional religions, which are pantheistic and involve ancestor and nature worship. Although worshippers may claim to believe in Islam, their day-to-day belief practices involve witchcraft, fetishes, and ancestral worship.

Christianity, of course, has many denominations. Further, numerous new religious movements (formerly called cults), claim to be Christian, but diverge from the historical orthodox form in essential doctrines. For example, the Latter-day Saints church (Mormons) is polytheistic, asserting that God the Father went through a process to attain the level of godhood and that humans can do the same.

Other worldviews that are derived from the main three include deism, which argues for one God as in theism, but the god of deism is not involved in the universe beyond creating the initial conditions, and so does not perform miracles. Agnosticism may be viewed as an offshoot of atheism in that agnostics believe that we cannot or do not know if God exists. There are other views as well, but for now we will focus on the main three worldviews.

A person's worldview can be identified by how she answers ultimate questions about life and human existence:

1. Origin questions deal with where the universe, biological life, and humans came from: how they originated. Atheistic worldviews argue that not only did the universe come into existence out of nothing, but also that all living things came into existence by blind, random processes. They believe that humans evolved through naturally occurring mechanisms from lower forms. Pantheists often believe the universe is eternal and evolves through unending cycles.

2. Identity questions seek to explain the nature of humans. Are humans merely complex animals that are higher on the food chain than other animals, as atheists would argue? Or, are humans divinely created in the image of their Creator, as Christianity, a theistic religion, proposes? Or, perhaps humans are merely transient entities that cycle through various forms, including animal forms, by way of numerous reincarnations, as Hinduism, a pantheistic religion, argues.

3. Meaning questions have to do with explaining the purpose of human existence. Atheism argues that this physical life is all there is. There is no ultimate meaning. As atheist scientist Richard Dawkins has famously said, "The universe that we observe has precisely the properties we should expect if there is, at bottom, no design, no purpose, no evil, no good, nothing but pitiless indifference."[15] Christianity counters that there is indeed an ultimate purpose to life, because as created beings, we were made in God's image and designed for eternal relationship with our Creator. For pantheistic religions such as Hinduism, a person's purpose for being here is to work off the debt incurred by *karma* and to ultimately reach enlightenment.

4. Morality questions deal with whether objective right and wrong exist. Atheists believe that morality is of our own making, a property of humans that aids in survival and that developed through natural selection. Christianity asserts that right and wrong flow from the nature of the supremely good Creator. He implants in humans a conscience, an awareness of right and wrong, as a natural aspect of man's being.

5. Knowledge questions have to do with whether reality by nature is knowable, and if so, to what extent and how humans can gain this knowledge. As pantheists, Hindus often believe that there really is no objective reality. What we think we see and know is actually *maya* or illusion. Another view on knowledge was espoused by agnostic philosopher Immanuel Kant, who asserted that we don't know things in reality (what he called "noumena"); we only know our perceptions created by our own minds (what he called "phenomena"). Conversely, Christianity asserts that things external to the human mind exist as part of the real world, and by nature are knowable.

6. Destiny questions focus on the ultimate future of humans. What happens to humans after death? Atheists argue that physical death is the end, and that there is no life after death. Pantheists often believe in *karma* and reincarnation, in which a person's actions in this life determine the organism, whether human or worm, into which a person will be reincarnated in her next life. While the ultimate goal is to reach *moksha*, a merging with Brahman, until a person has reached that level of enlightenment, she is destined to repeat the cycle of reincarnation.

Theists generally believe in an afterlife. For some forms of theism, such as Judaism and Islam, the destiny is determined by good works done here on earth. For the evangelical branch of Christianity, the destiny is determined by one's trusting or rejecting Jesus Christ's offer of salvation. Heaven is promised for all those who choose to trust Christ as Savior, while separation from God in hell is the final destiny for those who reject God's salvation through Christ.

Can All Worldviews Be True?

Pluralists are people who believe that many, if not all, religions or beliefs are aspects of one all-encompassing Truth. They will often say that all religions are just paths headed in the same direction: to the one God or one Truth. They also cite the well-known Blind Men and the Elephant parable to prove their point. As the story goes, six blind men touched an elephant, each coming in contact with a different part. One touched the side and thought it was a wall, another touched the tail and thought it was a rope, while another touched the tusk and thought it was a sword, and so on. Pluralists say that religions are very much like the blind men and the elephant in that each has one part of the all-encompassing Truth.

The problem is that all of the blind men were wrong, of course. It wasn't a rope, a wall, or a sword. If they had been sighted, they would have realized their error and recognized that it was an elephant. We can quickly debunk this misuse of an interesting ancient parable by observing that all religions cannot be true for one very simple reason: the religions or belief systems assert contradictory beliefs. And as we have learned, the Law of Non-contradiction demonstrates that two opposite beliefs cannot both be true.

I often hear pluralists says that all religions teach the same core beliefs. Actually, the opposite is true. Richard Howe, Christian philosopher and expert in new religions, as well as in world religions, has pointed out that in actuality it is the superficial beliefs of religions that are similar. Most religions teach "love your neighbor" and "do unto others as you would have them to unto to you."

But the essential or core beliefs are those beliefs that distinguish one religion from another. Evangelical professor of philosophy Ronald Nash (1936-2006) defines an essential belief: "A belief is essential to Christianity if its truth is a necessary condition for the truth of Christianity."[16] In other words, a belief is essential to a religion, if without it the religion would not be what it is.

Nash goes on to list essential beliefs of Christianity, including the belief that Jesus was God in the flesh, that He came into our world specifically to die in the place of humans for their sins, that the Father accepted His death in the place of humans as atonement for their sins, and that the acceptance of his sacrificial death in the place of humans was confirmed by His rising from the dead.[17] Not a single other religion in the world embraces these same core beliefs of Christianity.

When comparing the essential beliefs of Christianity about Jesus Christ with those of Islam, we see that for Muslims, the prophet Muhammad was the final prophet through whom God spoke, the Qur'an was his perfect message, and Isa (Jesus) was merely a good prophet. Further, Jesus did not die on the cross, nor did He rise from the dead. Hindus claim that God is the universe itself and that God expresses himself in multiple deities, of which Jesus may be just one of those incarnations (though he is not as great as Krishna).

All of these beliefs cannot be true since they are mutually exclusive. Jesus is either God or He is not. Let's not fool ourselves into thinking that all religions teach basically the same core beliefs. They don't. If they all taught the same core beliefs, distinct religions wouldn't exist at all.

The question then becomes how we discern which worldview or religion's claim about reality is true. That's what we are going to talk about in the next chapter.

10

If Cause and Effect, Then God

A. W. Tozer (1897-1963), author of *Knowledge of the Holy*, said, "What comes into our minds when we think about God is the most important thing about us."[18] Whether a person is an atheist, a pantheist, or a theist, she has personal beliefs about God. The importance of establishing God's existence with the skeptic as we walk them to the gospel cannot be overestimated. As Geisler says, "It makes no sense to speak about an act of God (i.e. a miracle) confirming that Christ is the Son of God and that the Bible is the Word of God unless of course there is a God who can have a Son and who can speak a Word. Theism, then, is a logical prerequisite to Christianity."[19]

Before we dig into the cause and effect argument, we need to talk about how to respond to atheists who insist that they simply "lack of belief" in God, or who say, "I just believe in one less God than you do." The reason they state it this way is to shift the burden of proof to the theist. The problem with saying that atheism is merely "lacking a belief," as apologist Frank Turek points out, is that to lack a belief is merely to talk about one's personal state of mind--a subjective mindset. The assertion doesn't respond to the question of whether there is a God. He adds, "Most people lack a belief in unguided evolution, yet no atheist would say that shows evolution is false."[20] Further, if merely lacking a belief in God makes someone an atheist, then a rat is an atheist. But saying animals and inanimate objects are atheists is incoherent, or at least irrelevant to the discussion.

Responding to those who argue that atheists just believe in one less God than theists is also fairly straightforward. Christian philosopher Richard Howe says, "Saying that as an atheist I just believe in one less God than you do is like saying that as an anarchist I just believe in one less government than you."[21] The gap between believing in no God versus no government and one God versus one government is gargantuan and is actually a difference in *kind*, not merely a difference in quantity.

Now we will examine good reasons for believing that God exists. We can engage both those who believe there is no God and also those who have misunderstandings about what *kind* of God exists, using three strong arguments that, when combined, provide overwhelming evidence that a personal Creator God caused and sustains the universe. What makes these arguments so helpful is the fact that even when we are talking with a person who does not believe the Bible is true, we have somewhere to direct the conversation. These are scientific and philosophical evidences congruent with the biblical record but that do not require us to cite Scripture (yet), since they are a part of general revelation: the created order.

Imagine talking to a university student who insists that she lacks a belief in God and that the Big Bang can account for everything that exists. Where do we go from here? The first line of evidence we may share is called the *cosmological argument*, but we will just call it the *cause and effect argument*. It is good, however, to know the word historically used for the argument, in case someone who has a philosophical background refers to the proper name of the argument. That way, at least we know to what they are referring.

Remember, in our discussion of deductive reasoning, we noted the unique way that deductive arguments are set up. We will now apply what we've learned about arguments to present evidence that God exists.

The deductive cause and effect argument goes like this:

1. Everything with a beginning has a cause.
2. The universe had a beginning.
3. Therefore, the universe had a cause.

We should memorize this deductive argument form. It is not hard to learn if we look at the pattern of the words and what they are claiming. We can share this argument in less formal wording in a conversation setting. We might say, for example, "Have you ever thought about the fact that everything in our universe, and the universe itself, began at some point? And since things that are not eternal are always caused by something else, the universe had to be caused by something else.

Since this is a deductive argument, if the conclusion logically flows from the premises (and it does), and both of the premises are true, then the conclusion is true. But are the premises true? That's the question. We need to look at the evidence to see if each of these premises is true beyond a reasonable doubt. Examining evidence that the premises are true employs inductive reasoning, often called the scientific method. If the evidence that the premises are true is beyond a reasonable doubt, it is rational to believe that a cause external to the universe produced it.

Everything with a Beginning Has a Cause (Premise #1)

Notice that the first premise does not say that everything has a cause. If something by nature is eternal, then it does not require a cause. Only things that *begin to exist* require a cause. As far as we know, everything in our universe, and the universe as a whole, began to exist at some point. In fact, the first premise states the *Principle of Causality*, a foundational scientific principle. We could not even *do* science if we did not believe that things that came into existence required causes, since that is what scientists do: look for causes of things. As Christian philosopher Peter Kreeft points out, "If there is no first cause, then the universe is like a great chain with many links; each link is held up by the link above it, but the whole chain is held up by nothing."[22]

Still, some people who hold science in awe argue that the universe could have popped into existence out of nothing, since, they say, quantum particles do so at the subatomic level. Of course, if things routinely popped into existence in the world we experience, we could expect hippos, computers, and Porsches to appear randomly in our living rooms from time to time, and while the Porsche might be kind of neat, I'm not all that excited about hippos.

Why would anyone think this could happen? Usually people of science cite the *Heisenberg Uncertainty Principle (HUP)* when they make the argument that since quantum particles can pop into existence without a cause, then maybe the universe did also. The HUP basically explains that we cannot determine both the speed (momentum) and the location of quantum particles simultaneously. But this principle does not deal with *causes* of the particles, it deals with our *ability* to identify their location and momentum both at once. They seem to pop into the energy field randomly. We can't pin them down. As astrophysicist Hugh Ross says,

> Quantum mechanics merely shows us that in the micro world of particle physics man is limited in his ability to measure quantum effects. Since quantum entities at any moment have the potential or possibility of behaving either as particles or waves, it is impossible, for example, to accurately measure both the position and the momentum of a quantum entity (the Heisenberg uncertainty principle). By choosing to determine the position of the entity the human observer has thereby lost information about its momentum.[23]

What causes this phenomenon? One possibility is that to observe these particles we must bombard them with electron microscopes, which may alter them in some way that accounts for their apparent randomness. But more significantly, when folks argue that they pop into existence "out of nothing," they equivocate on the meaning of "nothing." To equivocate on a term means to use it in two different ways, or with two different meanings, in a discussion or sentence. People making this assertion mean something different than what is usually meant by "nothing." An energy field into which the particles appear is not "nothing." It is "something": an energy field. The bottom line is that as far as we know, nothing cannot cause something.

You might be surprised at how far some people will go to prove that there is no God. Physicist Lawrence Krauss asserts that our universe, which he believes is flat, is the only kind of universe in which "the total energy in that universe is precisely zero" because "the negative energy of gravity balances out the positive energy of matter."[24] The upshot of this miraculous (*sans* God) state of affairs is that "the laws of physics allow the universe to begin from nothing. You don't need a deity. You have nothing, zero total energy, and quantum fluctuations can produce a universe."[25]

If you are thinking, I don't get it, since 1) the net amount of energy being zero does not translate into nothing existing, and 2) quantum fluctuations are something, you are in good company. Hugh Ross responded to Krauss's playing loose with the term "nothing" by saying,

Imagine someone throwing a shot put straight up in the air. There reaches a point in the shot put's trajectory where the upward kinetic energy exactly equals the downward gravitational energy. At that point, the shot put is moving neither up nor down. Its motion energy is zero. However, it would be wrong to conclude that the shot put is nothing. Even at that zero energy point, it is still a sphere of metal that weighs sixteen pounds.[26]

The same is true for the universe: zero net energy is not nothing.[27] Tucking away this example in our mental file cabinet will enable us to share with someone who makes the something-from-nothing argument.

Christian scientists are not the only ones to rebut Krauss's claims. Atheistic physicist David Albert also challenges Krauss's reasoning:

> Relativistic-quantum-field-theoretical vacuum states — no less than giraffes or refrigerators or solar systems — are particular arrangements of elementary physical stuff. The true relativistic-quantum-field-theoretical equivalent to there not being any physical stuff at all isn't this or that particular arrangement of the fields — . . . it is . . . the simple absence of the fields![28]

As we said, the energy field of quantum particles is not nothing. Notice here that we have cited a source who is not a Christian who disputes Krauss, someone in his own field of study. This is a very effective approach to use with skeptics. When Albert, who holds a similar worldview to that of Krauss, rebuts Krauss's claim, there can be no accusation of Christian bias and our counter arguments find more traction among skeptics.

Given the fact that "nothing" is nothing at all: no space, no time, no matter, then nothing exists that could cause anything. Therefore, the first premise stands, and while most will not argue with this first premise, for those who do, we have offered effective rebuttals. Let's move to the evidence for the second premise.

Evidence for the Universe's Beginning (Premise #2)

The second premise that the universe had a beginning is largely accepted by the scientific community, though this has not always been the case. Aristotle believed the universe was eternal, and Albert Einstein did also, which led him to make a catastrophic mathematical error that he considered the biggest blunder of his life, as he tried to accommodate an eternal universe in his calculations. But after looking at the overwhelming evidence for the universe's beginning, Einstein had to concede that the universe did, indeed, have a beginning.

Before we discuss evidences for the beginning of the universe, we need to discuss the differences and commonalities between old-earth creationist and young-earth creationist views regarding how the evidence is interpreted. Christians who hold a high view of Scripture—that Scripture is God's inerrant Word and that the Genesis creation account is historical—may differ in their views on the age of the universe. Young Earthers believe that the universe is thousands of years old, while Old Earthers believe that the universe is about 14 billion years old, as does the majority of the scientific community. Young Earthers discount Big Bang cosmology (which asserts that the initial event occurred randomly out of nothing), while Old Earthers (of which there are several versions) generally believe that the Big Bang occurred, but they reject the theory's assertion that it happened randomly.

But—and this is crucial—both Old and Young Earthers hold essential doctrines of the Christian faith in common and can be distinguished from heterodox views such as theistic evolution by these shared convictions. Despite the fact that Young Earthers often accuse Old Earthers of compromising on a high view of Scripture, both views offer strong arguments for some points, while needing to do more work in explaining certain other features of their views. Significantly, both believe that the universe and earth had a beginning, and that the beginning was caused by a direct act of God. Both believe that Genesis 1 and 2 reveal a historical account of creation.

The evidences presented below for the beginning of the universe are most often cited by Old Earthers; however, at some junctures most Young Earthers agree. The reason we are approaching this topic from more of an Old Earth perspective is simple. The vast majority of the atheists with whom we will talk will believe in the Big Bang and thus, that the universe is very old at about 14 billion years, with the earth being about 4 billion years old. Therefore, even if we hold to a Young Earth view, we will be able to meet them on their own turf to show that the universe had a beginning, and thus, requires a cause external to it.

Is this a compromise of faith? In my opinion, no. We might say, "Given *your* view that the universe is very old, there are several scientific reasons for believing that it had a beginning and required an external cause." Using the skeptic's own framework, we can show that even *if* that framework were accurate, the universe still had to have a beginning, and thus, a cause.

Doesn't a belief in the Big Bang presuppose that the universe had a beginning? Why do we need to even provide evidence for it? Janna Levin, a professor of physics and astronomy, like many other scientists who believe in the Big Bang theory (not the comedy show, the scientific model . . .), speculates that our universe is merely one of an infinite number. If the universe is part of an eternal process, then, of course, it does not require a cause. Two speculative theories that entail an eternal cyclical process, of which our universe's beginning is only one step, are the Cosmic Rebound Theory and the Multiverse Theory. Levin briefly describes both:

> It's possible that the universe was a bounce from a previous history when the universe was already big and started to collapse and bounced out into a new big bang, and then we were born in this cosmos that we think started 14 billion years ago, but really it goes back to infinity and eternity of bounces and cycles like this. Or it's possible that our universe is just one kind of bubble or plume off of a patchwork of other bubbles and plumes, and so there are other universes out there. It's like a mega-verse, but we can't contact them, so for all we know this is it; this is the whole cosmos.[29]

The short response to views suggesting our universe is only one of an infinite number of universes or an infinite number of rebounds is that this is merely speculation with no scientific support. Why do I call it mere speculation? Because Levin implies just this. As she points out, the only universe we are aware of is our own. Speculation about anything beyond our universe detours into philosophical discussion rather than scientific assertion supported by evidence.

While philosophical reasoning is certainly legitimate and also serves as a grounding and source of knowledge beyond (and beneath) scientific findings, it is scientists themselves (at least those who say the universe is all that exists), who argue that we cannot speculate about causes external to our universe. We must look only for natural causes within the universe. By their own pre-determined definition of science, when they discuss the possibilities that our universe rebounded from others or that our universe is only one of an infinite number of universes, they have made *un*scientific assertions.

Further, these explanations only kick the ball down the road, since the question of what caused the multiverse or the mega-verse remains to be answered. The upside of their speculations about the possibility of causes external to our universe is that doing so also legitimizes our assertions of a cause external to the universe. Now, back to the beginning. Several lines of scientific evidence show the universe had a beginning. Here are several.

1. Theory of General Relativity

One of Einstein's greatest contributions to the field of scientific knowledge, and for which he is most well-known, is his theory of relativity. The theory is actually comprised of two components: special relativity and general relativity. He first discovered the theory of special relativity, which asserted that the laws of physics "are the same for all non-accelerating observers" and that "the speed of light in a vacuum was independent of the motion of all observers."[30]

Ten years after Einstein developed the theory of special relativity he figured out how acceleration fit into the picture. His theory of general relativity deals with the relationship between space, time, and matter. He discovered that "massive objects cause a distortion in space-time."[31] We experience this as gravity, and it works like a bowling ball placed in the middle of a trampoline. The ball changes the curvature of the fabric into which it presses, and a marble rolled around the outside edge of the trampoline would circle downward toward the center.[32]

The interrelationship between space, time, and matter has implications for the issue of the universe's beginning. "General relativity tells us that what we call space is just another feature of the gravitational field of the universe, so space and space-time can and do not exist apart from the matter and energy that creates the gravitational field."[33] Therefore, space, time and matter are interdependent, or co-relative, coming into existence at once. Thus, the universe—space, time, and matter—had a beginning, and is not eternal.

2. Universe is Expanding

Another finding, actually noted by Einstein's contemporary, Edwin Hubble, provided evidence that the universe is expanding. What we mean by this, and what we need to explain, is that in the Big Bang model, galaxies are not expanding *into* space. Rather, space *itself* is expanding. Skeptical Einstein had to concede this reality when Hubble invited him to peer through the Wilson Observatory telescope. The phenomenon that confirmed the galaxies were moving away from us at a rapid speed came to be known as the "red shift." Simply put, in terms of the color spectrum, galaxies closer to us appear more toward the blue end of the color spectrum, while those moving farther away appear more toward the red end of the color spectrum. This is what Hubble discovered and what Einstein confirmed with his own eyes.

Red shift can be understood by way of a more familiar example. When a police car rushes by with sirens blaring as you stand on the sidewalk, the volume is loud and the pitch (frequency) is high. The instant it passes by, not only does the volume decrease, but the pitch lowers. This is called the Doppler Effect and is the audio equivalent of the visual red shift of galaxies as they move away from us.[34] Since the universe is expanding like a loosening coil, if we rewound the process, we would find that it collapsed back to a point of singularity, or nothing, showing that the universe had a beginning.

A high school student once asked me why the point of singularity could not be eternal. A Christian apologist friend who majored in physics, Prem Isaac, helped us understand why this could not be so. He explained that the laws of physics fail at the point of singularity, so, like speculation about multiverses, we can't scientifically study it. If the universe did begin with a point of singularity, there is agreement that matter/energy exploded outward. Given this fact, the point of singularity cannot be eternal, since if it were, it wouldn't make sense that it suddenly caused its own explosion.[35]

3. Second Law of Thermodynamics

The *Second Law of Thermodynamics* was discovered in the mid-1800s when scientists observed that heat did not tend to transfer from colder objects to warmer ones. Though the law is complex and involves more than the implications it has for the universe's origin, it shows that the universe is running out of *usable* energy, similar to how the batteries run down in a flashlight. Jim Lucas, a writer for Live Science, explains: "Processes that involve the transfer or conversion of heat energy are irreversible."[36] Though the total amount of energy remains stable in the universe (according to the *First Law of Thermodynamics*), as energy is used for work it is converted to an unusable form, resulting in a decreasing total amount of usable energy. Since this is the case, then there must be a limited, finite amount of energy in the universe, and the universe had to have a beginning.[37]

Another way of stating this law asserts that the universe and all that is in it moves from order to disorder. For this reason, the law is also called *The Law of Entropy*. This ubiquitous feature of the universe is obvious in our daily lives. Even the directions on Wikipedia for how to play the game Pick-Up Sticks explain that when the bundle of four different colors of sticks are dropped, they fall "in random disarray."[38] As a kid I knew that if I grouped the four colors of sticks into four corners in my hand according to their individual colors, once released, the sticks would fall into a random pile of colored sticks scattered in no particular order.

When interviewed by Lucas, physics professor Saibai Mitra, says about the movement from order to disorder, "At a very microscopic level, it simply says that if you have a system that is isolated, any natural process in that system progresses in the direction of increasing disorder, or entropy, of the system."[39] Though Old Earthers and Young Earthers would differ on its implication for the age of the universe, both affirm the *Second Law of Thermodynamics* as evidence that the universe had a beginning. Dr. Henry Morris, well-known for his work with the young-earth think tank Creation Research Institute, affirms that "in an isolated real system, shut off from external energy, the entropy (or disorganization) will always increase."[40]

Further, even if order increases in a specific location, Lucas affirms, "When you take the entire system including the environment into account, there is always a net increase in entropy (movement to disorder)." For example, says Lucas, while an evaporating salt water solution can produce more orderly crystals, "vaporized water is much more disorderly than liquid water. The process taken as a whole results in a net increase in disorder."[41] So, while I may increase order in a little corner of the universe by folding my clothes, it is at the expense of energy expenditure that always produces energy waste products, products that cannot be converted into usable energy.

The Logical Conclusion: The Universe Requires a Cause External to It

The whole point of explaining the evidence for things with beginnings having causes and the universe having a beginning, is to show the reasonableness of concluding that the universe itself requires a cause external to it. The cause of the universe cannot come from within it any more than a brick within a house can cause the house. But what kind of cause is required? Perhaps some nebulous non-personal force caused everything that exists.

One of the most fascinating and perplexing attributes of our universe is the existence of rational beings on earth. Given the fact that rational beings exist, the idea that a non-rational entity caused rational beings is unconvincing.

Further, whatever caused the universe must be personal since there was nothing and then something (the universe). This *change* in a state of affairs requires an act of will, a choice to cause or create. From these intuitively known truths we can reasonably infer that the kind of entity that caused the universe is extremely powerful and intelligent, and also possesses a will in order to choose to create. Since all things that exist are contingent (it is logically possible that they could *not* exist), there must be a personal cause who has chosen to sustain their existence moment by moment.

The final question often raised regarding the cause of the universe is, What caused God? When I talk with people I remind them that if the universe were eternal it would not require a cause. So, my claim that God does not require a cause since He is eternal and self-existent is not merely a God-of-the-Gaps argument, such that when I cannot give a natural explanation for something, I just say, "God did it." Rather, the evidence shows that the universe *did* have a beginning and requires an external cause. But, whatever caused the universe, if it is eternal, does not require a cause. Further, since time, space and matter came into existence all at once, whatever caused time, space, and matter must itself be timeless, spaceless, and immaterial. Theists call this being God.

11

If Order and Design, Then God

When we talk about the order and design of the universe and entities within the universe, we are basically referring to entities that exhibit complex patterns in structure and function that accomplish a purpose. These entities, from planets to microbes, act in predictable, or orderly, ways that have enabled scientists to identify patterns in nature we call natural laws. The intricate complexity of the universe is astounding, whether viewed through a telescope or a microscope.

As a nursing student in my twenties, I loved peering into the covert lives of bacteria invisible to my naked eye. Bacteria, as far as microbes go, are simple organisms. They have no nucleus and no organelles inside their membranes. Despite their simplicity, however, bacteria are hearty fellows, flourishing in diverse areas throughout the earth, including rocks, soil, and even in the arctic snow. One thing they are good at is replicating by a process called binary fission, in which one bacteria divides into two. At a suitable temperature and when provided adequate nutrition sources, bacteria such as *Escherichia coli* replicate themselves about every 20 minutes, meaning that in seven hours we will see 2,097,152 bacteria![42]

On a larger scale, when we look at the Grand Canyon we understand how mammoth natural forces produced the gorge. For a theist, natural forces are secondary causes that God uses to create. The water of the Colorado River and erosion produced the Grand Canyon. While God certainly was behind its magnificence, we readily recognize that the water and erosion account for the canyon, rather than thinking that God reached down and directly cut a gouge in the earth. However, if we were to travel to Wiltshire, England, we would see a structure called Stonehenge, that, though entirely stone, we would recognize as designed by intelligent beings (though it might still puzzle us as to how they did it!). When we look at structural patterns that yield certain functions in the stuff that makes up our universe, such as galaxies, gorges, or glia in our brains, we find that they bear the same tool markings of a sentient designer that Stonehenge or the Statue of Liberty bears.

The *order and design argument* is formally known as the *teleological argument*. Though the two are not identical, for our purposes they will be treated synonymously. Its deductive form goes like this:

1. Every design has a designer.
2. The universe shows evidence of complex design.
3. Therefore, the universe has a designer.

Every Design Reveals the Work of an Intelligent Designer (Premise #1)

In one episode of the popular crime scene investigation show called *CSI*, investigator Grissom finds a new body in the "body farm," an outdoor corpse library housing bodies in various states of deterioration. Normally, (if anything about a body farm could be considered normal), the forensic team examines the corpses to determine how various environmental variables influence the speed of decomposition. Their findings help them determine probable causes and times of death in specific homicides they are investigating. Of course, in this case, this particular body isn't supposed to be there, and the investigators use their forensic sleuthing skills to examine the circumstantial evidence in order to determine the cause of death.

Forensic scientists differ from experimental scientists in that forensic scientists seek causes of past events by examining evidence left behind, whereas experimental scientists seek causes for present events through experiments, in order to identify laws (patterns) in the way things work naturally in the world. Evolutionary biologist Josh Rosenau of the National Center for Science Education puts it like this: "Philosophers of science draw a distinction between research directed towards identifying laws and research which seeks to determine how particular historical events occurred."[43] He adds that philosophers of science "do not agree that historical claims are any less empirically verifiable than other sorts of claims."[44] In other words, this evolutionary biologist affirms that historical types of science are legitimate forms of scientific endeavors. Origin science, like forensic science, is a type of historical science, dealing with causes of past events.

Like forensic scientists, origin scientists who study possible causes for the origin of the universe, examine the effects—the artifacts left behind from past events—to determine the causes. Since historical sciences study artifacts, it is crucial to their methods and inferences that causes of events in the past are like causes of events in the present. This principle is called the *Principle of Uniformity* and is foundational to forensic and other historical sciences. So, if an archaeologist finds an ancient statue or pottery, he can reasonably infer that an intelligent being designed it, since all similar currently existing structures are caused by intelligent beings.

The principle of *Inference to the Best Explanation* enables scientists to hypothesize that the design requires a sentient designer of some sort. We use the principle every day. If you were to walk outside and see written in the dust layer on your car, "Clean me," you wouldn't think your cat jumped onto your car during the night, leaving a message. Rather, you would infer from the data—a specific instruction—that a person wrote on your car. Scientists use the principle all the time when they look for the best explanation available for the data they observe.

In the case of evaluating whether a feature of the universe implies an intelligent designer, Christian mathematician and philosopher William Dembski asserts, "We can legitimately infer design even if we know no details about the designer."[45] Even atheist scientist Richard Dawkins affirms that designed things bear identifiable characteristics. "Any engineer can recognize an object that has been designed, even poorly designed, for a purpose, and he can usually work out what that purpose is just by looking at the structure of the object."[46]

The Universe Shows Evidence of Design (Premise #2)

What are the identifiable characteristics that the universe and things within it display, which we can reasonably infer did not come into being by random, blind processes but rather by some sort of sentient being? Let's first look through the telescope and then through the microscope.

Design Visible Through the Telescope

The Anthropic Principle

We live on a razor's edge in terms of the precision required of certain cosmological variables in order for human life to exist on planet Earth. This feature of the universe came to be called the *Anthropic Principle*. Scientist Hugh Ross has done extensive research in this area, concluding:

> Now that the limits and parameters of the universe can be calculated, and some even directly measured, astronomers and physicists have begun to recognize a connection between these limits and parameters and the existence of life. It is impossible to imagine a universe containing life in which any one of the fundamental constants of physics or any one of the fundamental parameters of the universe is different, even slightly so, in one way or another.[47]

Human life would not be possible here on earth if cosmological parameters were not exactly what they are in the universe as a whole, in the galaxy, and also here on earth itself. For example, life could not exist here if:

1. the proton were not exactly 1,836 times more massive than an electron, since molecules would not form.

2. the expansion rate of the universe were slightly less, since the whole universe would have collapsed on itself, and if slightly more, no galaxies could have condensed and formed.

3. in our corner of the galaxy the average distance between stars were less or more than "about 30 trillion miles," since less would alter gravity interaction between stars, creating temperatures too extreme to support life, and if more, the orbits of the planets would be altered so that earth could never even have developed.

4. earth's axial tilt were any greater or any less, since "surface temperature differences would be too great" to support life.

5. the "ratio of reflected light to total amount falling on surface" were different, since if it were greater there would occur an uncontrolled ice age and if less, an uncontrolled greenhouse effect, either of which would prohibit life from existing on earth.[48]

While many more anthropic constants could be cited, this brief list alone is enough to confirm that the margin of error is extremely small for both parameters in the universe and also for those on our earth. One final observation by Ross demonstrates the significance of the *Anthropic Principle*. Ross is a Christian scientist who holds to the old-earth view, asserting a universe age of about 14 billion years old and calculating earth's age at about 4 billion years old. Even if the universe and earth are that old, Ross says,

> The universe is at least ten billion orders of magnitude too small or too young for life to have assembled itself by natural processes. These kinds of calculations have been done by researchers, both non-theists and theists, in a variety of disciplines.[49]

The debate here is not whether the universe is billions or thousands of years old. Even *if* the earth is four billion years old as Old Earthers argue, there still is *not enough time* for natural, undirected processes to explain the emergence of life.

Design Visible Through the Microscope

1. Specified Complexity

William Dembski is known for his work in calculating the mathematical boundaries for the probability of certain features of our world coming about by natural, undirected causes as opposed to intelligent beings. In explaining what he means by specified complexity, Dembski gives an example that distinguishes among things that are specific but not complex, things that are complex but not specific, and things that exhibit both characteristics and therefore require a sentient designer.

A letter of the alphabet, says Dembski, is *specific* but not complex, because it is a single unit representative of a larger group that follows an independently formed pattern (all the other letters constituting an alphabet). Conversely, a long list of random letters is *complex*, requiring complex instructions to formulate, but it is not specific because the letters in the set are not presented in a pre-formulated pattern. One of Shakespeare's sonnets, however, would qualify as both specified and complex and thus, displays evidence of being designed.[50] The implication of this principle, says Dembski, is that in "all cases where we know the causal history and specified complexity was involved, that an intelligence was involved as well. The inductive generalization that follows is that all cases of specified complexity involve intelligence."[51]

One feature of all living cells exhibits specified complexity and thus, can be reasonably attributed to an intelligent designer. The double-helix of DNA located within the cell's nucleus was discovered by James Watson and Francis Crick in 1953. Fifty years later, in 2003, Francis Collins' team completed mapping of the human genome. A genome "is an organism's complete set of DNA, including all of its genes. Each genome contains all of the information needed to build and maintain that organism. In humans, a copy of the entire genome—more than 3 billion DNA base pairs—is contained in all cells that have a nucleus."[52]

A brief descriptive excerpt by Collins helps us understand how DNA exhibits specified complexity:

> The outside backbone is made up of a monotonous ribbon of phosphates and sugars, but the interesting stuff lies on the inside. The rungs of the ladder are made up of combinations of four chemical components, called "bases." Let's call them (from the actual chemical names of these DNA bases) A, C, G, and T. Each of these chemical bases has a particular shape.
>
> Now imagine that out of these four shapes, the A shape can fit neatly only on a ladder rung next to the T-shape, and the G-shape can fit only next to the C-shape. These are 'base pairs.' Then you can picture the DNA molecular as a twisting ladder, with each rung made up of one base pair. There are four possible rungs: A-T, T-A, C-G, and G-C. If any single base is damaged on any one strand, it can be easily repaired by reference to the other strand: the only possible replacement for a T (for example) is another T. Perhaps most elegantly, the double helix immediately suggests a means of its self-copying, since each strand can be used as a template for the production of a new one. If you split all the pairs in half, cutting your ladder down the

center of each rung, each half-ladder contains all the information needed to rebuild a complete copy of the original.

As a first approximation, one can therefore think of DNA as an instructional script, a software program, sitting in the nucleus of the cell. Its coding language has only four letters (or two bits, in computer terms) in its alphabet. A particular instruction, known as a gene, is made up of hundreds or thousands of letters of code. All of the elaborate functions of the cell, even in as complex an organism as ourselves, have to be directed by the order of letters in this script.[53]

DNA, in other words, is no random sequence of letters, but rather yields information, a message, just as our 26-letter English alphabet does, when organized in specific patterns. The only difference is that DNA's alphabet has only 4 letters. So, DNA is not analogous to a language; it *is* a language. Language, because it is informational, is only produced by sentient beings. Never in our world have we seen language produced by random processes; therefore, we can infer from the pattern of DNA that it, too, is designed by an intelligent being.

But DNA is not the most convincing microscopic biological evidence of design. A few years ago, at the National Conference on Christian Apologetics in Charlotte, North Carolina, I sat mesmerized in a workshop presented by Dr. Tom Woodward, DNA researcher, who asserted that as complex and wondrous as DNA is, the epigenome has upstaged it in complexity. If DNA comprises the instruments in an orchestra, said Woodward, the epigenome is the director and music that tells the musicians what to play.

As we have noted, every cell has the same patterned DNA structure and the same genes, which are sections of DNA that do certain work. So how do cells differentiate in order to do different work in the body, as in a lung cell, an eye cell, or a skeletal muscle cell?

The difference between cells in different tissues and organs is that the "expression" of the genes differs between cells. Expression means that the message from the DNA is being copied and made into protein. For example, liver cells have different proteins than skin cells, even though their DNA is the same.[54]

So, then the question becomes, What controls the expression of genes? That is, what turns them on or off? Woodward says that we can look to the epigenome for part of the answer. "Epi" means above, so the epigenome is above or beyond (actually hiding in plain sight right alongside) the DNA, and Woodward gives a peek at its microscopic magnificence:

> Researchers have discovered a complex system in the cell—sophisticated "software" situated beyond DNA—that directs DNA's functions and is responsible for our embryonic development and the differentiation of a single, fertilized egg cell into more than two hundred cell types in a mature body. . . . It guides the expression of DNA, telling different kinds of cells to use different genes, and to use them in the precise ways that meet the needs of those different cells. This "information beyond DNA" plays a crucial role in each of our sixty trillion cells, telling the genes exactly when, where, and how they are to be expressed.[55]

Explaining more about how the epigenome works, Woodward says,

> The histone code is extremely important to understand how DNA functions, how it's read, how it's copied, how it's shut down. . . . The histone code is . . . a series of three small chemical attachments to the tails. There are actually eight tails that stick out from the histone spool where DNA is wound up on. There's about 30 million of them in a typical nucleus. And these histone spools have like landing strips for special little chemical markers and there are sockets built into the side of those tails, and as the various acetyl, phosphor, or methyl tags are added, it sends signals both to the DNA control system and to several other molecular systems residing in or near the nucleus, and then DNA is then locked down or . . . it's opened up. It's sometimes primed for special kinds of activities. It's amazing that this code sat right beside the DNA code and science never knew it existed until . . . 15 years ago. Then there's the methyl code. Methyl tags are attached directly to DNA. . . . And then we find information inscribed even on the cell membrane and some of the structures

in the cell. . . . The zygote code is staggering. The fertilized egg has its own code. Information is inscribed everywhere.[56]

If reading the information on the complexity of DNA and the epigenome leaves you dazed, welcome to the club. A master's degree in nursing, including microbiology courses, does little to keep this information from hitting the air just over my head. But that is the point. If we come away with anything after reading these descriptions, it is the fact that the microcosm of the intracellular world is communicating information at a rate and depth that staggers the imagination. And the epigenome, the intracellular master control system that orchestrates the activities of the DNA, is even more intricate than the DNA itself. This control system acts on the DNA by sending messages about exactly what to do, and it differentiates cells' jobs. If that were not enough, here's the kicker:

> If one envisions the epigenome's role as the orchestra director of DNA, this is a director with metaphorical "eyes and ears." This biochemical conductor is sensitive to his biological environment. The quality of his directing can be changed as he picks up signals that tell him what is happening in the body's tissues and organs. For example, he can be strengthened in his daily work with a sensible diet, which supports his efficient DNA-directing, or he can be damaged and poisoned through binging, which leads to sloppy and even fatal waving of his wand.[57]

We have always been told that our DNA is what it is, and we can't change it. So, our family histories dramatically impact the types of diseases we develop. But while we can't change our DNA, we *can* change how it works, and unlike DNA, acquired changes in epigenetic information can be transmitted to the next generation.

So, while sadly I cannot change my DNA tendency toward high cholesterol thanks to my family history, I can change how my epigenome impacts DNA's functioning to improve my health. Moreover, some of these changes can be passed on to children I bear, if I engage in healthy activities prior to childbearing years. Discovery of these exquisitely complex multi-layered microsystems catapults evolutionary explanations of their origins beyond the reach of naturalistic biologists.

2. Irreducible Complexity

One stormy night the electricity goes out in your house. You feel your way to the kitchen where you rummage around in a drawer to find your trusty flashlight. Finding it, you click the switch on and are relieved that the light comes on. The lens covering the light is broken out, but otherwise it looks like it's in good working order.

Your simple flashlight is made of a case that holds the parts; a lamp that serves as the light source; batteries that serve as the power source; a strip of metal that enables electrical contact between the batteries, lamp, and switch; and the switch to activate the flow of electricity. [58]

You recognize that while the missing flashlight lens is needed to protect the lightbulb, it is not essential to the functioning of the flashlight. However, once the lens is gone, no part of the flashlight can be removed and still preserve the flashlight's function. Every single part—the case, the lamp, the batteries, the strip of metal and the switch—must be structurally correct and present in its correct location, all at once, for the flashlight to function at all. In other words, the flashlight's component parts are *irreducible*, so that if you remove any one part (try to reduce it), the flashlight will not work.

Biochemist Michael Behe originated the concept of irreducible complexity. He argues that the origin of things that display the characteristic of irreducible complexity cannot be explained by natural, gradual evolutionary mechanisms; rather, they require the direct intervention of a sentient designer. While he affirms that not all subcellular biological systems show evidence of design, many do. And some cry out design in the form of an irreducible kind of complexity.

The cilium, for example, is "a structure that, crudely put, looks like a hair and beats like a whip."[59] Cilia are located in places such as in the fallopian tube where they function to move the egg along its route from the ovary through the fallopian tube. What are the parts of its basic structure and how do those parts work together to fulfill a function that efficiently utilizes all the parts? Behe explains:

> Ciliary motion certainly requires microtubules; otherwise there would be no strands to slide. Additionally it requires a motor, or else the microtubules of the cilium would lie stiff and motionless. Furthermore, it requires linkers to tug on neighboring strands, converting the sliding motion into a

bending motion, and preventing the structure from falling apart. All of these parts are required to perform one function: ciliary motion. Just as a mousetrap does not work unless all of its constituent parts are present, ciliary motion simply does not exist in the absence of microtubules, connectors, and motors. Therefore, we can conclude that the cilium is irreducibly complex—an enormous monkey wrench thrown into its presumed gradual, Darwinian evolution.[60]

The significance of Behe's findings is that cilia, like all systems that use the motion of paddling to get from one place to another, whether we are talking about a boat that moves by a propeller or a cilium,

> fail if any one of the components is absent. . . . The complexity of the cilium and other swimming systems is *inherent in the task itself.* It does not depend on how large or small the system is, whether it has to move a cell or move a ship: in order to paddle, several components are required.[61] [Behe's italics]

Of course, opponents of Behe's views have quickly fired back that perhaps evolutionary mechanisms can indeed account for the development of cilium through alternative work-around routes, "perhaps adapting parts that were originally used for other purposes."[62] The problem is that during the process in which parts that originally performed other functions were being modified for their new role, they would not yet be able to perform the new function.[63] They are sort of in limbo. For evolutionists this is an insurmountable problem, because naturalistic mechanisms require that the changes occur gradually, in tiny steps, and each step of the way, every miniscule modification must provide a survival advantage to the organism in order for natural selection to preserve it.

Therefore, the Universe Has a Designer (Conclusion)

We have affirmed that things with a design, that is, an informational pattern of structure that enables a certain function, are not produced by random, unguided processes, but require a sentient designer. Looking through the telescope we have seen that the *Anthropic Principle* reveals that the universe, our galaxy, and our planet display cosmological parameters that allow for only a narrow range of variability for life to exist, and yet, those parameters came about and are maintained so that life exists here on earth.

Looking through the microscope we find that living systems display specified complexity in that they have structural patterns that convey information, as well as many exhibiting irreducible complexity, so that if any one part of a system is missing it will not work at all. The emergence of these systems cannot be explained by gradual, step-by-step processes, since each step of the way, the change in a part would have to enhance the survival of the organism; yet, as we have said, the system won't function at all if even one part is missing. Thus, these attributes call for a designer and cannot be accounted for by blind, unguided natural processes, such as those suggested by Darwinian evolutionists.

Based on the *Principle of Uniformity* that says that causes in the past are like causes in the present, given the fact that the sorts of things presently that display these attributes of order and design require a sentient designer, the *Inference to the Best Explanation* enables us reasonably to conclude that the universe, the galaxy, the earth itself, and the things within it, required a designer to come into existence and to continue to exist with all the life-sustaining constants currently intact.

Our evidence supports what Scripture already affirms. Through the telescope we see that "the heavens declare the glory of God, and the sky above proclaims his handiwork" (Psalm 19:1). Through the microscope we see that "my frame was not hidden from you, when I was being made in secret, intricately woven in the depths of the earth. Your eyes saw my unformed substance" (Psalm 139:13-16a).

12

If Right and Wrong, Then God

You are sitting quietly in a restaurant eating your overpriced sandwich and shake, listening to music with your earbuds tuning out all other noises: in short, bothering nobody. Over walks a gal who stares at your plate for a moment before grabbing the other half of your sandwich, then ambling to a nearby table, only after taking a swig from your diet soda. More than miffed you get up and walk to her table. Before going ballistic, you have a moment's reservation. What if the woman is hungry and can't buy food? So, you say, "What's going on? Why did you take my sandwich?" She replies, "It looks good. I just wanted it." Your jaw drops open and you can't think of a reply. Everything in you screams to pop her in the nose. Why? Because you know what she is doing is wrong. It's unfair.

Spend five minutes in a classroom of fourth graders and you will find that a sense of justice reigns. "Hey, that's mine. You can't take it." "That's not fair." "You're mean." "You should share." "You shouldn't say those mean things. You might hurt her feelings." "Teacher, I didn't get as many crackers as Joey did." And on it goes. The idea of fairness and justice is ubiquitous and is evident even in children. Now, notice I didn't say children acted fairly. Their sense of fairness is usually most acute when someone wrongs them, not vice versa (pretty much like adults). Nevertheless, even my four-year-old grandson gets sheepish when pressed as to whether he told the whole truth about how many cookies he ate when mom wasn't looking.

We will see the same feature if we visit the U.S. legislature. A common misconception abounds that we cannot legislate morality. In fact, that is exactly what we do legislate. Our lawmakers sponsor bills that legislate legal actions, defining them as right or wrong, and the judicial system enforces those laws with penalties for disregarding them. You want to run a red light because you have some place important to go? Because you have jeopardized not only your life but also the lives of others, you will suffer the penalty because what you have done is wrong. It is true that we cannot legislate motivations and desires. But we do indeed make laws based on those actions that we believe are moral and those that are immoral.

Many people deny that objective morality exists. Atheistic philosopher J.L. Mackie (1917-1981) insists, "There are no objective values," and he includes in "values" morality.[64] Does this mean that values are merely a social construct that was developed so that society will survive, and my grandson feels guilty only because he has been trained to do so? Those of us who hold a theistic worldview argue, No. There's a lot more to the story. The existence of an awareness of rightness and wrongness about things that is intrinsic to human personality signals that a designer has been at work.

What is formally called the *moral argument*, we also call the *right and wrong argument*. Its deductive form goes like this:

1. If there is an objective moral law there is a lawgiver.
2. There is an objective moral law.
3. Therefore, there is a moral lawgiver.

Moral Laws Only Arise from Beings that *Make* Laws (Premise #1)

The first reason we can know that moral laws only arise from moral beings (lawgivers) is that moral laws are not the same as what we call natural laws. Natural laws such as gravity merely describe the patterns we see in the universe. Moral law, unlike natural law, carries with it a sense of ought-ness, not just is-ness. In other words, moral laws tell us what we should do, not just what we actually do. These ought-to kinds of laws universally arise from sentient, morally aware kinds of beings.

Second, unlike animals, humans are uniquely hardwired to appraise certain actions and attitudes in terms of rightness and wrongness. You will never see a wolf acting conflicted in the remotest sense about eating alive a mother rabbit's newborn baby bunny. While it is true we can train dogs to cower when they do something we don't like, this is not the same feature as the feeling of gnawing guilt and remorse often evident in humans when they harm someone else or act selfishly. Moral laws, then, are produced by thinking, moral beings who possess the aptitude for and sensitivity of moral awareness. They never arise by chance or from inanimate objects.

There Is an Objective Moral Law (Premise #2)

Atheists and other skeptics offer several explanations for the existence of what appears to us as moral law, but really is not. They often argue that a universal moral law does not exist because what is right and wrong differs across societies and therefore must be relative to people, time, and place. In some societies, showing the sole of the shoe is considered an offense, whereas in other societies it is irrelevant. Does this mean that morality is relative? No. In both cases the root issue is respect for the dignity of humans. The two cultures may disagree on *how* to show respect, but both value human dignity.

One of the greatest Christian thinkers and apologists of the twentieth century, C.S. Lewis (1898-1963), argued that moral laws actually show remarkable consistency across societies. After all, he said, if we looked at many societies we would find that none of them lauded cowardice in the soldier who abandoned his comrades in battle.[65] No one thinks it is right to beat babies for entertainment. So, there are universal standards accepted by virtually all societies.

Another argument often raised by atheists is that what appears to be the moral law is simply a survival mechanism, a socially learned behavior. Atheist philosopher Michael Ruse says, "Morality is just an aid to survival and reproduction."[66] Therefore, says Ruse, "Morality is an ephemeral product of the evolutionary process, just as are other adaptations. It has no existence or being beyond this, and any deeper meaning is illusory."[67] In Ruse's way of thinking, what appears to be a universal moral law actually aids in the survival of the tribe or community and thus, propagation of the species, which is what we would expect with natural selection.

Lewis is of great help in responding to this argument, as well. He affirmed that the "herd" instinct predisposes us to protect those we love or who are members of our group. But, he also observed that the moral law cannot be an instinct itself since it arbitrates between two instincts: the instinct to help others and the instinct to preserve one's self. So, when someone is drowning, for example, I may instinctively want to help the person, but quickly my self-preservation instinct kicks in. It is the moral law that enables me at times to decide to act against my own natural instinct of self-preservation and risk my own safety for the sake of another.[68]

Finally, to those who suggest that the understanding of right and wrong is merely a socially learned behavior, we respond that just because a behavior is learned it does not necessarily mean that it is *merely* a learned behavior. As Lewis pointed out, we teach children multiplication tables, but these mathematical principles existed as an inherent feature of the universe before they were learned.[69]

Lewis himself understood the mindset of the skeptic, having been a staunch atheist who came to faith because of his reflection on the moral law. His journey to Christianity was littered with questions about God's goodness:

> My argument against God was that the universe seemed so cruel and unjust. But how had I got this idea of just and unjust? A man does not call a line crooked unless he has some idea of a straight line. What was I comparing this universe with when I called it unjust?[70]

Lewis' point is well-made. How do we get the idea of injustice except as a foil to justice, or the idea of evil except as the antithesis of good?

The Need for an External Source in Order to Define "Good"

Every year in my senior high school apologetics class, when we came to the discussion of objective morality, I showed a video clip of Christian apologist and author Frank Turek talking to an atheist college student named Kyle. Kyle was an atheist and a really nice guy. Turek demonstrates what to say in order to show that an objective moral law must exist and that the existence of a moral law shows there is a God. He also demonstrates how to argue a point graciously, with patience and persistence, as we walk people to the gospel. (Look on crossexamined.org to watch the video.)[71]

As you read the dialogue below, observe Kyle's reasoning. Also, notice how Frank patiently reiterates why it is true that without God there can be no objective moral law. And if moral law is merely subjective, then personal opinion reigns and there can be no real right or wrong.

Kyle to Frank Turek: You asked why someone would be an atheist. . . . There's so many terrible things in the Bible. Like, at one point, Jesus says to his disciples, it's great that they are torturing their slaves, but only lightly, you know, even though they did nothing wrong. . . . I don't understand why you would want to want to follow such a God. . . .

Frank: Let's not even look at the context of that passage. Let's just assume that what you said is 100 percent true, okay? As an atheist, why is that wrong?

Kyle: Why is that wrong? Morally I would think that each and every human being here is the same. We all have the same rights. We all have the same wants, needs. . . .

Frank: But you seem to be assuming that certain things are really right and people have certain rights, even if there is no God. How do you justify that? What's your standard of rightness?

Kyle: My standard of rightness would be a fair society.

Frank: What do you mean by fair?

Kyle: Everything is equal. . . . All humans should be the same.

Frank: So, it's your thought of fairness. What if Hitler has a different idea of fairness—is he wrong?

Kyle: He's not wrong.

Frank: Hitler's not wrong?

Kyle: Well, I think we should take the utilitarian view, whatever is best for the most amount of us.

Frank: But what do you mean by "best"?

Kyle: The greatest positives for the most amount of people.

Frank: But you are assuming that there's a "best" out there. You are assuming a moral law. Where does that moral law come from if there's no God?

Kyle: I personally just think that human beings should be able to make up their own laws. Each people in time have found their own moral laws. And I personally think they get better and better over time.

Frank: But you wouldn't even know what "better" was unless you knew what "best" was. So, I'm asking you, What is your standard of "best" to say that certain people are closer to the "best" or "better" than others? What's the standard? Is it just your opinion or is there something beyond your opinion that says, This is good?

Kyle: We've all heard about utopias and a perfect society, . . . there's no murder. . . .

Frank: But . . . what's wrong with murder if there is no God? Why shouldn't I kill people to get what I want?

Kyle: Because it doesn't help society.

Frank: But why should I care about society?

Kyle: Because as a group we should care about society. We should be making a betterment of ourselves.

Frank: But, Kyle, you are importing a moral law into a frame that has no moral law. As an atheist you are trying to say there is no God, which means there is no standard of rightness out there. But I'm saying this is my own personal standard of rightness, which means someone could come along like Hitler or Stalin, and say, "Kyle, if there's no standard of rightness beyond either you or me, then I can do whatever I want, including killing you to get what you have."

Kyle: It's a very good point. . . . I don't think that God is needed in a sense. I'm not looking for perfection . . . I am looking for human beings simply to work together to better society. I don't see a need for a perfect identity up above.

Frank: I'm not saying an atheist can't be a good person. I'm not saying atheists don't know right from wrong. . . . My point is that it seems difficult to justify what rightness is if everything is reduced to human opinion. Which human gets to decide? . . . If there is not an external referent to say that this is good and this is evil, then we're all just here and we're fending for ourselves.

A lot of people will say we need to cooperate to get along. Actually, that's not true. Take someone like Stalin; he cooperated with very few people, just his henchmen, and he killed twenty million people to get what he wanted . . . . So, the problem it seems to me is, we know . . . what's right . . . and I don't need to believe in God to know that. I just need there to *be* a God to justify it. . . .

A lot of atheists say I know right and wrong, and I agree, you know right and wrong. But that's like saying, I can know what a book says and deny there's an author, which is true. But there would be no book to read unless there was an author. The same is true when it comes to morality. You can know what the right thing to do is and deny there's a God, but there would be no right thing to do unless there was a God.

This conversation shows us that Kyle persisted in using terms borrowed from the theistic worldview, a worldview that asserts objective morality exists: fair, right, better, best, good. Frank consistently brought this to his attention by asking him the question, What do you mean by "fair" and "better"? Slowly, the light began to dawn, and Kyle recognized that given his atheistic worldview, there was no such thing as right, wrong, better, good, perfect, and no obligation to help society, if each person got to decide what was right.

His convictions about the rightness and obligation to better society was a chimera, and had no grounding whatsoever without a referent external to humans. The truth is, though, that most people really do believe some things are right and some things are wrong. No one lives as though right and wrong do not exist at all, especially when they believe that their own rights and dignity have been violated.

Therefore, there is Moral Lawgiver External to Humans (Conclusion)

We have shown that the moral law is different than natural laws in that the moral law carries with it an idea of ought-ness by asserting what we should do, not by just describing what we actually do. Also, moral awareness is unique to humans, but is absent in animals. Thus, we can say that if the moral law does indeed exist, it arose from a thinking, moral kind of being, not from supposed lower forms or from nature itself.

We have also submitted for consideration the evidence that a universal moral standard does exist. To those who would argue that it is merely an instinctual survival instinct, we respond that it cannot merely be an instinct since it stands as judge over our instincts, guiding us at times to act against our own self-interests. Moreover, just because morally right actions can be learned does not prove that the principles undergirding them did not already exist, just as mathematical principles exist before we teach them to our children.

Further, as Kyle and Frank's conversation demonstrates, the moral law must have originated from an external referent. If the moral law is relative to persons, we could never say the mass murders committed by Stalin or Hitler are wrong; they are merely an expression of those persons' own definitions of what is right. Moral law cannot merely be defined as what helps society survive either, since many leaders cared nothing about cooperating to do what was best for society, and in fact, annihilated massive sectors of their own population group.

Finally, the moral law could not have originated in humans for one very simple reason. While all of us as humans believe certain actions and beliefs are really right and others wrong, not a single human lives a perfectly moral life. As Lewis observed, while all humans know the moral law, each and every one of them fails to keep the law.[72] Therefore, it is reasonable to believe that since moral law had to arise from a moral kind of being, and since there is a universal moral law, there is an external Moral Lawgiver as the source of the moral law.

Philosophical reasoning leads us to the same conclusion as does Scripture. Objective moral law exists, and humans are answerable to God Himself for knowing and doing good:

> Woe to those who call evil good and good evil, who put darkness for light and light for darkness, who put bitter for sweet and sweet for bitter! Woe to those who are wise in their own eyes, and shrewd in their own sight! Woe to those who are heroes at drinking wine, and valiant men in mixing strong drink, who acquit the guilty for a bribe, and deprive the innocent of his right! (Isa. 5:20-23).

Further, what is morally right is not arbitrarily defined by God; rather, goodness is His nature. Since this is true, humans can know the good by knowing God. "Oh, taste and see that the Lord is good! Blessed is the man who takes refuge in him!" (Psalm 34:8).

13

If Evil, No God?

Several church friends and I drove to a neighborhood where we hoped to find and welcome a family who had visited our church. We knocked on the door, but no one answered. Not wanting to waste the trip, we went next door to see if the neighbor had any spiritual needs or wanted to visit our church. A middle-aged woman answered. We introduced ourselves and asked about her spiritual concerns. She answered, "I am so depressed. I believed in God. But not since 9-11. That changed everything. Now, I just don't know. I don't see how a good God could let that happen. I just can't believe that God exists anymore."

What is called the problem of evil is likely the most often raised objection to the truth claims of Christianity. How can a good, all-powerful God exist and evil also exist? The two seem contradictory. This leaves us with an untenable alternative. God is all-good and would stop evil if He could, but He can't. But if He can't stop evil, is He really worthy of worship? Or maybe God is all-powerful and could stop evil if He wanted to, but He doesn't. This alternative seems worse since our option now is to worship a cruel, uncaring, and perhaps even malicious deity.

Another troubling question is whether God created evil. Even we as theists believe that evil is not eternal since it originated with Satan and angels, who are created beings. Given the fact that all things that come into being must be caused by something external to them, it would seem that we are left with the conclusion that God created evil.

How we think through these issues and the convictions we share with the disbeliever about evil may impact how she responds to God.

We can prepare to respond redemptively to someone who comes to us seeking insight into her own pain and sorrow, and who longs for hope. When I say "redemptively" I mean that we can respond in such a way as to bring the truth to bear upon the issue, so that the individual is led to the gospel. Moreover, how we answer these questions influences the stability of our own faith and what happens to our faith when tragedy tears the very fabric of our hearts.

The Green Glob of Evil?

Before we tackle how both evil and God could exist, we need to agree on what evil is. Atheism, pantheism, and theism offer differing explanations of the nature and origins of evil. Some atheists, such as Richard Dawkins, whom we quoted earlier, insist that evil does not exist. Of course, Dawkins does think that parents forcing their religious beliefs on their children is *bad*,[73] and atheists often cite the existence of evil as the reason they don't believe in God. Pantheists often view evil as an illusion, and yet they acknowledge that this world is getting worse and worse.

From a theistic perspective, Thomas Aquinas (1225-1274), Christian philosopher, theologian, and Catholic priest, asserted that while evil is real, it is not a thing (a substance with properties), like a green glob floating around and out to get us (not Aquinas's words exactly). It does not exist in its own right. Rather, evil exists only in good things. It is derivative. So, it would have no identity on its own without the good substance's existence. This is what is meant when we say that evil is a lack of good, or a privation of good.

> As the term "good" signifies perfect being, so the term "evil" signifies nothing else than privation of perfect being. A thing is called evil if it lacks a perfection it ought to have. Thus if a man lacks the sense of sight, this is an evil for him. But the same lack is not an evil for a stone, for the stone is not equipped by nature to have the faculty of sight. [74]

Good in its basic sense, then, is not being nice or kind. Good is perfection of existence, completely fulfilling one's design or nature. In helping high school students understand this concept, I often used the analogy of a hole in a fence. The hole in the fence is analogous to evil, because it is a lack of something—"fence-ness"—that is supposed to be there, if the fence were fulfilling its intended natural design as a perfect, or complete fence. Holes in Swiss cheese are not an evil since the holes are an aspect of the cheese's natural and perfect state (plus, since the holes result in fewer calories, that has to be *good* . . .).[75]

Evil: Where Did It Come From?

In the view of Christian theism, evil entered our world through the created being known as Satan. We are not told in Scripture how evil came about in Satan, only that evil was found in him, if we take Ezekiel 28's lament for the King of Tyre to also refer to Satan, as many scholars do. In Ezekiel 28:13 he is called an "anointed guardian cherub" who was "in Eden, the garden of God." Then, in verse 16 it simply says, "You were blameless in your ways from the day you were created, till unrighteousness was found in you."

Genesis 3 records Satan's tempting Eve and Adam, who as moral beings, had been endowed by God with the (good) perfection of free will, or the power of moral choice. This good gift of free will was misused by Adam and Eve to rebel against the God who created and loved them. Therefore, humans themselves are personally responsible for evil.

Genesis 3:16-19 records how sin impacted physical bodies, the relationship of husband and wife, and the natural world. Woman would experience pain in bearing children. Instead of the husband leading and the wife joyfully yielding to his leadership, the wife would fight for control, and the husband would seek to dominate or "rule" her. Man would fight for every grain stalk to feed his family as the soil became unresponsive and instead of yielding crops, produced thorns.

Romans 8:20-22 suggests that evil altered the physical state and functioning of the universe:

> For the creation was subjected to futility, not willingly, but because of him who subjected it, in hope that the creation itself will be set free from its bondage to corruption and obtain the freedom of the glory of the children of God. For we know that the whole creation has been groaning together in the pains of childbirth until now.

The Fall, then, does not merely account for moral evil, as many skeptics argue. Instead, a predominant view among evangelical Christian theists is that Romans 8 describes a corruption of the entire created order, also producing natural evil.

Is God Obligated to Stop Evil Now?

Some skeptics argue that if God did exist, He would stop evil now. But since humans do evil through free will, not only would God have to annihilate free will, but also humans themselves. When someone says to me that God should stop evil, I can respond, "Should He start with you?" Most people are far less gung-ho about God stopping evil when they realize that in their minds, the concept of evil is always out-there rather than in-here. We need to be less concerned about the evil that happens *to* us than the evil that happens *through* us.

Also, to say that God has not stopped evil yet is not to say that He will not defeat evil in the future. Norman Geisler and Joseph Holden, authors of teen apologetics book *Living Loud*, point out that in the Christian theistic view, Christ has already *officially* defeated evil on the cross and He will *actually* defeat evil at His return.[76]

To clarify the distinction between the terms "official" and "actual" I often share the story of how we adopted our daughter, Neli, who lived in an orphanage in Mexico until age three, when we met her on a medical mission trip. It took us about 10 months (my longest pregnancy) to complete the process of adoption, including home studies, working with immigration offices in the U.S. and in Mexico, as well as completing all the paper work and consultations with the lawyer. Once the adoption papers were signed, she was legally our daughter. The adoption papers said so. But we still could not bring her home from Mexico until the visa came through. It took three more agonizing months before the visa was in our hands. Once we had it in our possession, we drove all night from Louisiana to Mexico and brought her back across the border to our home in Louisiana, where she physically lived with us. So, when the adoption papers were complete Neli *officially* became our daughter, but when she entered our home she *actually* became our daughter.

So, it is with Christ's defeat of evil. He has done all that must be done. The fate of sin and death are sealed. The Cross said so. Still, we await the reality of Christ's return when the defeat of evil will become actual.

Could God Have Made a World with No Evil?

For God to create a world with no evil, He would have had to make humans robots. Real love results from real choices. For God to make humans without the ability to choose to do right or choose to love, may have produced a world without evil, but it also would have been a world without love or freedom. An amoral world consisting of only rocks, cats, and other non-moral things is not a better world. In this world there would exist no relational, emotional, or intellectual kinds of beings.

Some skeptics have countered that God could have made a world in which all people freely chose to do only good. Not all Christian philosophers think this is even logically possible. Geisler reminds us, though, that just because a state of affairs is *conceivable*, it is not necessarily *achievable*. "As long as everyone is really free, it is always possible that someone will refuse to do the good."[77] Otherwise, says Geisler, we have a situation in which people are forced to do good via "forced freedom." To force good negates good. God could, of course, not create that person, but then again, that is saying that non-existence is better than existence. Further, in some sense, creating a world where people only did what was right would deprive us from developing virtues that come about only as we respond to evil.[78]

Does All Evil Have a Purpose?

Many Christian theologians argue that while evil is not good, the way God is able to use it in his sovereign plan to accomplish His ultimate purpose *is* good. He has even revealed to us some of those purposes accomplished through evil in specific situations. When I read the story of Joseph in Genesis 37-45, I feel deep compassion for this young man who was a victim of what we now call human trafficking, when his brothers sold him to traders on their way to Egypt. Finding himself in a foreign culture, he was faithful to God in an excruciatingly difficult situation. He eventually acquired a good position with a government official, only to be falsely accused of a crime, and ended up in jail.

Through God's providence, after his release Joseph arose to a position of authority over the land, second only to Pharaoh. This was a fortuitous turn of events for his family, the same brothers who sold him. For when they arrived in Egypt seeking to buy food because of the famine in Israel, it was Joseph who saved them. The patriarchs of the 12 tribes of Israel survived to spawn a nation though whom Messiah, the Savior of the world, would be born.

Scripture gives many accounts of evil that occurred which, in the hand of God, was transformed to do God's will. The Bible says God even uses evil kings to accomplish His purposes (Dan. 2: 20-21, Psalm 75:4-7, Prov. 21:1, Rev. 17:17).

Must every evil that occurs accomplish a greater good purpose to mitigate God's culpability for evil? Geisler says, No. "Just as when a blacksmith hammers the molten iron into a horseshoe, resulting in some wayward sparks, that do not have a specific purpose," so is it the case that "only the general purpose needs to be good" in order for God to use this world as "the best possible way to attain his ultimate goal of the greater good."[79]

Another Christian philosopher, Bruce Little, takes a different approach in his *Creation Order Theodicy,* a theodicy being an explanation of exactly how God could be sovereign and loving, and still allow evil. He argues that when God created the world, He endowed creation with a certain order in which man has real freedom to choose and to experience the consequences of his choices.

While God is sovereign, He is sovereign in the sense that a father oversees his family and the rules in the home, without ordering each member to do certain things, like a dictator. God could intervene and does so at times, but He is not obligated to do so. Thus, when evil occurs, it is not so that a greater good comes about. In Little's view, requiring a greater good would make God responsible for evil, since God would need evil in order to accomplish the greater good. Instead, gratuitous evil, or evil without a greater purpose, does occur. "God lets some things play out in history, because that's the way He constructed the world—He respects His creation."[80]

Hope in Suffering, Holiness in Character

Suffering intrudes in many forms. Just yesterday a well-known Christian apologist tweeted that he had to step down from ministry due to unexpected illness. I learned that he had just been diagnosed with a condition that he will not survive unless the Lord providentially intervenes to save him. A former student of mine regularly posts on social media the number of months since her week-old baby girl died from a medical condition that went undiagnosed for several days. One of my dearest friends awoke one day perfectly fine, only to be paralyzed from the waist down by evening. She was eventually diagnosed with West Nile virus that has put her in a wheelchair for the past two years.

I have no answer to the whys that scream for answers in each of these precious ones' experiences. Suffering is the bane and the blessing of human existence. We easily appraise it as the first, and only when pressed as the second.

For each of the individuals I just mentioned, suffering has come just as a result of living in a fallen, broken world. None of them did anything wrong for which the natural consequence brought on the malady. But even a cursory look at suffering in our own lives and the lives of others reveals other causes of suffering, as well. Sometimes we suffer for our own foolish decisions that bring painful consequences.

In my teen and early adult years I loved swimming and being outside in the sun. The problem is that I have skin designed for England and Scotland where the sun doesn't shine nearly as much. I freckle like crazy, and my hope that the freckles would all run together and make a great tan has long since faded. I now must routinely check with my dermatologist who examines my skin and then burns, freezes, or cuts precancerous lesions off my skin. Yuck. But this is the natural consequence of foolish decisions I made in the past.

Of course, by comparison, these consequences are not nearly as serious as others I have suffered at the hands of my own immaturity and rebellion against the Lord, but am too embarrassed to share in these pages. We all have these stories of suffering that comes as a result of our own foolish or even sinful decisions.

Though less common in my own life, suffering can also come from doing good and acting righteously. The Lord Jesus serves as the epitome of someone who suffered for righteousness' sake. If we look at 1 Peter 3:15, our banner scripture on apologetics, we find that the mandate to prepare ourselves to give a defense of the hope within is actually embedded in a larger passage on suffering for righteousness. Verse 16 even promises that when we share the reason for the hope within we can count on being slandered and criticized.

And then in verses 17 and 18 Peter says something crucial to experiencing joy within the kind of suffering that results from righteousness: "For it is better to suffer for doing good, if that should be God's will, than for doing evil. For Christ also suffered once for sins, the righteous for the unrighteous" (1 Peter 3:17-18a). Our hope and joy when we suffer for goodness' sake is knowing that we participate, or join with, Christ in His suffering, which He gladly embraced for our sake.

I said that I had no answer to the whys of those who suffered. But even though we most commonly ask why in our pain, asking who may be more helpful. When I am in agony, I find one solace that soothes my questioning mind more than any other, and it's found in Isaiah 53:5-6:

> But he was pierced for our transgressions; he was crushed for our iniquities; upon him was the chastisement that brought us peace, and with his wounds we are healed. All we like sheep have gone astray; we have turned—every one—to his own way; and the LORD has laid on him the iniquity of us all.

When I talk to people hunkered down in the throes of grief, pain, or guilt, and they ask me, "Why did God let this happen?" I can say that I don't know. But this I do know. I know who opened the gate to suffering. And He is not the angry God who zaps us every time we make a misstep. He is the God hanging on the tree with arms open wide, embracing the justified wrath of holy God for our sins. He has promised to never leave us or forsake us, even when our pain comes as a consequence of our own sin. Instead, He stands ready to forgive that for which He has already paid, if we turn in repentance to Him. And He will walk with us and sustain us through the pain until we get to the other side, regardless of the source of our pain.

We can also know that if we choose to know Him in the suffering place, He will accomplish good through it. James 1:3-4 promises that "the testing of our faith produces steadfastness," the full effect of which is our maturity's completion.

When my dad was dying a few years ago, tears were never far from spilling down my cheeks as I watched his struggle with pain and trying to breathe. One day I told him, "Daddy, I am so sorry that you are hurting like this. But I cannot pray that the Lord take you home one minute before He says it is time. For whatever His reasons are, I trust that He is working your sanctification through this and making you ready for heaven." We can trust that God is bringing about the holiness for which our hearts cry even when, and perhaps most when, we yield to Him within our weakest and most helpless moments of deep suffering.

In this chapter we have made an initial attempt to respond to the question of whether it is reasonable to believe God exists in light of the evil in the world. We have seen that evil is not a thing; rather, it is a lack of something good. While the theist may seem to have the most difficulty answering the question, it is only because the other two major worldviews deny evil or blame the God-who-isn't-there for evil.

We are not left without response to the one who claims God cannot exist because of evil. The fact is, the presence of evil makes the existence of God necessary. For evil cannot exist apart from good, and good does not exist, as we have seen in the chapter on morality, without God.

If humans have been endowed with real choices that have real consequences, then Christianity offers the best explanation for the existence of evil in the world—both moral evil and natural evil—and frames evil in the light of eternity. When it is all said and done, the Cross provides the best response to evil. There Christ paid for sin, conquered evil and death, and purchased our eternal hope with His own blood, confirming the final word that evil is temporary and Christ has defeated it.

14

If God, Then Miracles

As we embark on a discussion of whether miracles are possible, we need to review how we arrived at this juncture through the logical progression of arguments. Remember, we started with providing evidence for the existence of truth, then offered arguments for God's existence, then for Jesus' deity. More specifically, we first presented evidence that objective truth exists, and thus, truth cannot be relative and subjective. We then presented strong evidence that it is the theistic kind of God who exists, using the cause and effect, order and design, and right and wrong arguments.

Our conclusion is that it is reasonable not only to believe that God exists, but that the kind of God who exists is ultimately powerful and intelligent, and is the very essence of goodness. He is even able to use evil to accomplish His purposes. This rules out the possibility that atheism, pantheism (e.g. Hinduism), and polytheism (e.g. Mormonism, because finite gods require a cause), can be true.

Further, there can only be one of these infinite Beings because for there to be two infinite Beings would require that they differ in some way (something to distinguish them). In whatever way they differed, one would lack something and therefore, would not be infinite. Thus, we are left with the three great monotheistic religions of the world as possible contenders for being the one true worldview. How do we discern which religion is true? By looking to see in which religion God has intervened supernaturally in the natural world to confirm His message and messengers.

Since God created the kinds of beings called humans who were designed for relationship, it makes sense that He would initiate relationship with them, revealing Himself through interventions in the natural world. Otherwise, He could have just stopped creation at cats, who are only relational when they want something.

The issue of whether miracles are possible is critical to the truth claims of Christianity. We claim that Jesus Christ miraculously came to earth as God in the flesh in the form of a human baby, performed miracles of healing, controlled nature, and even raised someone from the dead. Most importantly, we claim that He died and physically arose from the dead three days later, conquering death, gaining our spiritual freedom from sin, restoring our relationship with God, and guaranteeing our future hope of heaven.

If miracles are not possible, we might as well throw our Bibles in the trash on the way out the door, because Christianity is not Christianity without miracles. Our goal here is not to show that Jesus' miracles were authentic. Before we can do that we must explain how it is rational to think that miracles are even possible.

What Are Miracles?

His name is John of God and thousands flock to him in Brazil, seeking "the best-known healer of the last 2000 years."[81] Despite no medical training, he has purportedly treated some 15 million people over the past 40 years. His tone is humble: "I do not cure anybody. God heals, and in his infinite goodness permits the Entities to heal and console my brothers. I am merely an instrument in God's divine hands."[82] His interventions include corneal scrapings and nasal probing, and he proposes to heal not only physical ailments but also fear and materialistic mindsets.[83]

Miraculous claims capture our imagination and offer hope for the ailments of this life. But what exactly are miracles, are they rationally possible, and how do we distinguish real miracles from fakes? For the apologetics purpose of breaking down barriers that intellectually block someone from considering the gospel, it would seem that a claim for the possibility of miracles would actually stymie our efforts. In our culture's worship of science and the scientific method, many do not believe there is room for the miraculous in rational thinking.

There is little consensus regarding the nature and definition of miracles. For John of God, a definition of miracles involves opening himself as a medium to immaterial spirits and to dead saints who work through him as an instrument of supernatural healing. He says that they use his mind and body; he serves as a medium through whom they work.

Australian philosopher J.L. Mackie (1917-1981), whose atheistic convictions did not allow for God, defined miracles as an intrusion from outside the known natural world: "The laws of nature, we must say, describe the ways in which the world—including, of course, human beings—works when left to itself, when not interfered with. A miracle occurs when the world is not left to itself, when something distinct from the natural order as a whole intrudes into it."[84]

According to the Christian theistic view, miracles are supernatural acts in which God intervenes in the natural order to reveal Himself. Biblically speaking, by definition, the purpose and character of miracles are confined to those acts that bring glory to God and are consistent with His nature and His revelation. Many miracles were used by God to confirm His message and His messenger to mankind. In other words, they are authenticating acts God uses to make Himself known to humans.

If Natural Law, No Miracles?

Charles Darwin recorded in autobiographical notes that during his voyage on the Beagle he had already begun questioning the veracity of the Old Testament, largely because of its miraculous claims. After giving it some thought, he says, "The clearest evidence would be requisite to make any sane man believe in the miracles by which Christianity is supported. . . . The more we know of the fixed laws of nature the more incredible do miracles become."[85] Even if God did exist, the likelihood of miracles became increasingly implausible for Darwin. In his mind, natural law precluded their possibility.

Deists and David Hume would agree. Deists, unlike theists, believe that God does exist, but that He is not active in the day-to-day world. He wound up the clock of the universe, pushed start, and went to lunch. Natural laws that He set in place run on their own and preclude the possibility of miracles. Skeptic philosopher David Hume (1711-1776) died the year America was born as a nation, but his views dominated for more than 200 years. He was not a fan of the miraculous. Hume argued that miracles were a violation of natural law. Natural laws are regular, he said, and miracles by definition are rare events. Since evidence for regular events (natural law) is always greater than that for rare events (miracles), a wise person should not believe in miracles.

There are several flaws in this reasoning. First, if we apply the principle of believing in the regular rather than the rare, then events that most atheistic scientists believe occurred are not believable, by their own rules. The Big Bang that produced our universe, for instance, if it occurred, happened once. We have no evidence otherwise, and so we should not believe it occurred, or that any one-time event in our lives or in history occurred.

Second, it simply isn't true that evidence for all regular events is greater than for rare events. On March 26, 1953, physician Jonas Salk, announced during a nationally broadcasted radio show that he had "successfully tested a vaccine against poliomyelitis."[86] If we applied Hume's rule, we would not believe it, despite the fact that the evidence showed it did work. All first-time discoveries are single, rare events. Should we not believe them?

Third, to argue that someone doesn't believe in natural law because she believes miracles can occur is unreasonable. The fact that I believe miracles are possible presupposes that I believe natural laws exist. Otherwise, I could not recognize the exception to the usual pattern. As Church of England clergyman and scholar William Adams (1706?-1789) said, "There must be a regular course of nature, before there can be any thing [sic] extraordinary. A river must flow before its stream can be interrupted."[87]

C.S. Lewis weighed in on the possibility of miracles in his book, *Miracles*. He observed that physicists claim that the "smallest particles," by which I take him to mean sub-atomic particles, move "in an indeterminate or random fashion."[88] We discussed this phenomenon called the *Heisenberg Uncertainty Principle*, noting that some skeptic scientists do indeed argue for the randomness of sub-atomic particles. If this were true, says Lewis, then these really small particles act independently of natural law. They do not function as an interdependent piece of the larger puzzle, so to speak.

Here's where it gets interesting and is applicable to our discussion of the possibility of miracles, which are *super*natural events. On their own view, then, these scientists are suggesting that these particles, since they "do not interlock with all other events," says Lewis, "are not part of Nature. . . [but rather] sub-natural.[89] Lewis argues that once the door is open into the universe from *sub*-nature, there is no reason to exclude as wishful thinking or fairy tale, the possibility that a door opens into our world from the *super*-natural, thus, allowing for the possibility of miracles.

Perhaps naturalists, who believe that nature is all there is, would argue that what appears to be sub-nature is actually a part of our natural world, but we just don't know yet how that part works. Fair enough. But, on the other hand, since these same scientists assert that the pattern of natural law is unchangeable, and these particles do not fit the pattern, at this time they do not act in the deterministic fashion required to qualify as part of the natural order, by their own definition.

When we consider whether miracles are possible, the issue always comes back to God. If the theistic God exists, and we have already provided strong evidence that He does, then miracles must be possible. For a theist believes that God already performed the greatest miracle, creating everything from nothing. He also created the forces that act within the universe that make it predictable and allow us to function within it. We have recognized these patterns as natural law. It is also reasonable, then, to think that God would intervene in recognizable ways within His created order to reveal His nature, His power, and His purpose. We call these interventions, miracles.

Distinguishing True Miracles from Fakes

In order to identify an event as a miracle, it must fulfill the *purpose* of a miracle. Miracles, as biblically defined, were performed for the expressed purpose of revealing the One, True God. In the case of John of God, investigations suggest he is a charlatan, but even if he sincerely believes in what he is doing and does so with good motivations, his methodology is antithetical to scriptural teaching, which forbids channeling. Deuteronomy 18:10-12 is clear:

> There shall not be found among you anyone who burns his son or his daughter as an offering, anyone who practices divination or tells fortunes or interprets omens, or a sorcerer or a charmer or a medium or a necromancer or one who inquires of the dead, for whoever does these things is an abomination to the Lord. And because of these abominations the Lord your God is driving them out before you.

Therefore, what he claims to be miracles of God cannot be true miracles. He may be using sleight of hand, which we call magic, to trick people. Further, because people want so badly to be healed, there may be a psychosomatic component to the responses some people claim as healing. Or, it is possible that he is actually opening himself to demonic activity, which would be super*normal* but not super*natural*, since angels are a part of the natural created order. Thus, his interventions can in no way be construed as miracles.

In explaining how to recognize true miracles, Geisler describes miracles as distinctive in several dimensions. A miracle's *unnatural* dimension, such as seeing a burning bush that is not consumed, draws attention. A miracle's *theological* dimension requires that the kind of God who can perform miracles exists. When a pantheist says that a miracle occurred, we can be sure that it is not a miracle, as biblically defined, since the pantheist's definition of "God" contradicts the theistic definition. Its *moral* dimension reveals God's moral character. Its *teleological* dimension affirms God's purposes to bring glory to Himself and to benefit His creation. Miracles were never performed to entertain or merely impress. They were performed to bring people to God. So, when people claim to do miracles through channeling or any anti-biblical method, they cannot be of God. And "confirming" kinds of miracles in Scripture had a *doctrinal* dimension in that they confirmed truth claims.[90] For instance, Deuteronomy 18:22 mandated that when a prophet claimed to be God's spokesman and an event he foretold did not happen, the prophet's words were not from the LORD. God has provided us, then, with markers of true miracles, so that we may distinguish between true and fake miracles.

Did Muhammad Perform Authenticating Miracles?

In August 2015 the first installment of a film trilogy, "Muhammad, the Messenger of Allah," was released in Iran, says Ayman S. Ibrahim, a professor of Islamic Studies at Southern Baptist Theological Seminary. Presenting the Shi'ite version of Muhammad, and opposed by Sunni Muslims, the movie "was packed with miracles performed by Muhammad."[91] What is strange about this, says Ibrahim, is that this directly contradicts the Qur'an, which clearly says Muhammad did not perform miracles.

The Qur'an teaches about itself that it is self-authenticating, providing its own proof that God is its source. Many Muslims argue that the Qur'an is the only miracle needed to prove that Muhammad is God's prophet and Islam is the only true religion. According to surah 29:51, the evidence of the Qur'an should be enough to warrant belief: "And is it not sufficient for them that We revealed to you the Book which is recited to them? Indeed in that is a mercy and reminder for a people who believe."[92]

Several passages specifically say that Muhammad did not perform miracles. Surah 17:59 explains that miracles were not provided because they had previously been rejected. People even questioned why Muhammad did not perform miracles, according to surahs 6:37, 13:7, and 28:48. Some argue that while the Qur'an omitted miracles, they were recorded in other sources, such as Hadith, (collections of Muhammad's sayings and deeds compiled over time).[93] But as Ibrahim notes, "If other later religious texts, nonetheless, seem to suggest that Muhammad did perform miracles, they stand in direct opposition to these verses, among many others, in Islam's scripture."[94]

Miracles Then and Now?

Miracles have not occurred regularly throughout history. In the Bible miracles clustered around the eras of Moses, the Old Testament prophets, and were prevalent in the lives of the New Testament apostles and Jesus Christ.

In the Old Testament, the book of Exodus records numerous miracles performed by Moses and Aaron, including the plagues on the nation of Egypt and opening of the Red Sea. These miracles confirmed that Moses was God's spokesperson, and that the Israelites would prosper only when they listened to and obeyed his instructions, which came straight from God.

Miracles occurred in the lives of the prophets such as Elijah (1 Kings 18), when God sent fire to consume the sacrifice on the altar, so that the people would listen to God's message through Elijah and turn from worshipping Baal. Elijah and others who held the office of prophet both foretold God's events to come and forth-told God's message. The requirement of Deuteronomy 18:20-22 held prophets to a high standard. If they spoke anything not directed by God, or if they foretold an event that did not come true, they were to die.

The era when Christ performed His ministry on earth and the apostles lived was also characterized by miracles. Peter and John performed miracles that healed the sick, for example, and confirmed their gospel message as from God. Christ brought the New Covenant, a new message, and God authenticated Him and His message with miracles.

When people ask me do I think miracles occur today, I have to respond that they may. God can perform a miracle any time He wishes. I tend to think though, given the purpose of miracles, that they are less needed today. We now have the written Word of God, and miracles occurred most often during times when the full written Word was not available, in order to authenticate a new message from God.

If miracles occur today, they are most likely to occur in areas of the world where the Scripture is suppressed. Though I have not personally encountered miracles (though I have experienced God's providential work in my life many times), I know missionaries whose accounts I trust, speak of them occurring in situations they have seen or have been reported to them by other missionaries. Numerous reports have emerged from access-restricted countries in which someone dreams or has a waking vision of a man who tells them how to find Jesus.

No doubt God will use whatever intervention necessary to reach someone whose heart will respond to the gospel. He did so with Cornelius in Acts 10. He sent an angel to direct Cornelius to Peter, so he could hear the gospel message. At the same time, He revealed to Peter a vision that helped him understand that the Gentiles were to be included in the family of God.

We have discussed reasons for believing miracles are possible. If the theistic God exists, miracles must be possible, for He has already performed the greatest miracle: creating everything from nothing. It also makes sense that He would reveal Himself to humans whom He created and loves. While skeptics such as Hume argue that miracles cannot occur, there is no reason to think that God cannot suspend natural law, employ unknown natural laws, or intervene in nature any way He sees fit in order to bring glory to Himself and to accomplish His purposes in history.

Part 4

Talk About Jesus

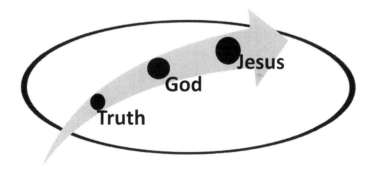

15

Can We Know What the New Testament Writers Wrote?

So far our apologetic conversation has taken us through two major topic areas: Truth and God. We have established that objective truth does exist. Based on this fact we offered evidence that the theistic kind of God exists. Since the theistic God is a personal, Creator God beyond the universe yet active in the universe, there is good reason to think He would make Himself known through supernatural acts called miracles. Christianity supplies more evidence by far for miraculous occurrences, and stands alone in its evidences of unique supernatural acts that bring glory to God and confirm His message.

The New Testament documents serve as the major source of information on Jesus Christ's life, including His miracles, His words, His death, and His resurrection. Therefore, it is vital to know how accurately we can reconstruct from the manuscripts (ancient handwritten copies) what the writers wrote in the autographs (the originals that were distributed to the churches). Once we have confirmed that we can confidently reconstruct what the originals said, then we need to investigate to what extent we can trust what the writers of the New Testament said was true. We are not yet attempting to show that the New Testament is inspired by God. Once we establish that Jesus is God, He will affirm that in His own words.

The reason we focus on the New Testament rather than the Old Testament at this juncture is that the Old Testament is called into question less often. Further, the salvation message and claims of Christ's identity as God are clearly asserted in the New Testament. Once the trustworthiness of the New Testament is confirmed as reliable, Christ Himself confirms the Old Testament in His own words.

We have no originals available for examination, as far as we know. This should not alarm us, for we have no originals for any other ancient documents, either. The absence of originals comes as no surprise, given the fact that they were distributed among the churches and likely copied to the point of disintegration.

My New Testament professor at Southeastern Baptist Theological Seminary, David Alan Black, says that textual criticism is the discipline by which scholars seek to "recover the original text from the available evidence."[95] He also explains that textual critics examine three kinds of materials: Greek manuscripts, ancient versions, and the writings of early church fathers who were scholars in the early church.[96]

Textual critics study all kinds of ancient documents, not just the New Testament. So we can evaluate how the New Testament fares in terms of reliability by comparing its documents with those of other ancient writers. The first step in determining reliability has to do with our ability to reconstruct from the existing copies the original wording of the text. Several principles guide textual critics in determining original wording based on extant (existing) copies only.

Numerous Copies Enable Verification of Original Text

For most ancient Greco-Roman texts we have a handful (and for some, none) up to a few hundred copies. The ancient writer for whom exists the greatest number of copies is Homer. According to evangelical scholar Daniel Wallace, of the Center for the Study of New Testament Manuscripts,

> The average classical author's literary remains number no more than twenty copies. We have more than 1,000 times the manuscript data for the New Testament than we do for the average Greco-Roman author. . . . The very best classical author in terms of extant copies is Homer: manuscripts of Homer number less than 2,400, compared to the New Testament manuscripts that are approximately ten times that amount.[97]

Wallace confirms that more than 5,800 handwritten ancient Greek New Testament manuscripts have been catalogued (and the number is rising as more are found).[98]

In addition to translations in Greek, the New Testament was also translated into numerous other ancient languages such as Latin, Coptic, and Syriac, of which we have tens of thousands of copies. bringing the total number to more than 20,000. Most manuscripts do not contain the entire New Testament. While even a verse or two (such as the John Rylands fragment) counts as a manuscript, the average length of most manuscripts, says Wallace, is 450 pages long.[99]

But what about the differences in the readings of these manuscripts? Differences are called variants, and agnostic Professor of Religious Studies at UNC Chapel Hill, Bart Ehrman, is right that there are more variants in the manuscripts than there are words in the New Testament. There are about 140,000 words in the New Testament and the number of variants among New Testament ancient manuscripts ranges from 200,000 to 400,000. This sounds ominous for the Christian who believes in the trustworthiness of the New Testament. But Daniel Wallace notes that Ehrman and others' implication that we cannot reconstruct the New Testament wording because of so many errors is misleading.[100]

For one thing, as author of *Textual Criticism of the Bible* Paul D. Wegner notes, there is *no question* about the vast majority of the New Testament text. "The fourth edition of the United Bible Societies'. . . *Greek New Testament* text notes variants regarding. . . only about seven percent of the text."[101] This means that 93% of the text is undisputed. Thus, the vast majority of the New Testament's original wording is uncontested.

For the remaining 7% of text for which there are variants, examining the *kinds* of variants gives us a clearer picture. Wallace categorizes the variants into four types:

a. Spelling and nonsense readings account for 75% of the total number of variants. They are easily detectable and affect nothing.

b. Changes that can't be translated and synonyms, as well as word order changes due to the flexibility of the Greek that affect emphasis, but do not affect meaning.

c. Meaningful variants that are not viable are those variants with meaningful differences, but a good case for their being the actual original wording cannot be made.

d. Meaningful *and* viable variants account for less than 1% of the total. They do affect meaning, but none affects an essential belief of orthodox Christianity.[102]

Thus, for most variants in the remaining 7% of the New Testament text containing differences, we can identify the original wording, and these variants have little to no impact on the meaning of the text. Less than 1% impact the meaning of the text, and *not a single one* has wording that would call into question an essential belief of Christianity. For example, in Mark 9:28-29 the disciples ask why they could not cast out a demon, and Jesus responds, "This kind cannot be driven out by anything but prayer." Some ancient manuscripts add, "and fasting." Though the meaning of this text is certainly impacted by which reading is correct, whichever one is correct does not change any essential belief of our faith.[103]

Another misunderstanding relates to how the manuscript content was transmitted. Many people falsely assume that New Testament transmission mimicked that of the telephone game in which information is passed from one person to the next in a linear fashion, with each person getting his information only from the one previous person in the line. New Testament text transmission, however, occurred through multiple lines, so that one document was likely copied several to many times. This pattern of transmission would be more like a grandmother writing a recipe that each of her eight daughters copied individually, with the 18 granddaughters copying their mothers' copies. The multiple lines of transmission of the New Testament produced families of manuscripts that proliferated in certain areas of the world and could be compared with other families of manuscripts. Often what one is missing another fills in and many differences can be quickly identified and the original wording restored.

Finally, even with multiple errors the original wording can often be easily reconstructed. For example, if yu slitl wdoner how teh ograiirnl wdnriog cluod be rsetroed wtih so mnay errros, try raiendg tihs! Most people are able to figure out what the sentence says, even in this garbled form. You can use this example to explain to someone that we can usually restore original wording with confidence, even with multiple errors in a text.

The accuracy of the New Testament we hold in our hands is unparalleled when compared with other ancient documents. Nevertheless, we do not want to minimize the complexity of the task for textual critics in reconstructing disputed passages whose variants do affect the meaning of the text.

But nor should we overreact to these challenges. Most modern English translations mark or provide footnotes for significant disputed passages. So, readers are alerted to difficulties in confirming the original reading of certain texts or to questions about whether a passage was in the original.

The fact is, many readers have never even noticed them (for instance, look in your Bible at the bracketed notations at the end of John 7 and Mark 16:9-20). As more manuscripts are discovered, Wallace anticipates that we will continue to get closer and closer to the original wording for those texts for which there are significant variants. And for the bulk of the text, there is no question whatsoever about what the originals said.

Older Copies Are Nearer the Time of Original Writing

When compared to the works of any other ancient writer, the time gap between the original New Testament writings and their earliest copies is far less. Daniel Wallace says, "The extant manuscripts of the average classical author are no earlier than 500 years after the time he wrote. For the New Testament, we are waiting mere decades for surviving copies."[104]

Until 2011, the earliest New Testament manuscript was the John Rylands fragment (called P52) of John 18:31-33, 37-38, dated to about A.D. 125, only about 30 years after John lived. Other manuscripts exist from 25-150 years after the original eyewitnesses lived and wrote. Contrast the John Rylands fragment's early date with Homer's and Livy's writings for which the earliest manuscript witness is about 400 years after the original writings.[105]

In his 2012 debate with Bart Ehrman, Daniel Wallace announced that "as many as six more second-century papyri" fragments have been discovered. (Remember, the second century starts in A.D. 100, and Christ and the eyewitnesses lived in the first century). One is from Luke's

Gospel and is dated to about the same time as the John Rylands fragment.

But the most significant is a fragment from Mark's Gospel, "which a leading paleographer has dated to the first century."[106] We have no other Mark manuscript even dated as early as the second century, which Ehrman had already pointed out earlier in the debate, so understandably, Wallace's claim has fueled a lot of speculation in the press and drawn criticism, with many scholars expressing skepticism that this fragment is an authentic first-century document.

Wallace himself cannot speak about details at this time. But professor Denny Burk, who teaches in the college of Southern Baptist Theological Seminary, says in a January 19, 2015 blog that he has "heard from Daniel Wallace privately, and he stands by his original claims from the debate with Ehrman."[107] Why go into such detail about a manuscript not yet fully vetted? Its significance would be monumental, for as Wallace notes, this document may have been written "while some of the first-generation Christians were still alive and before the New Testament was even completed."[108] We await further confirmation as the documents are studied and their status reported in the literature.

A Chain of Custody Raises Confidence that the Original Text Was Preserved

Ehrman would have us believe that we cannot know who wrote many of the New Testament books, even asserting some were forgeries. Cold case homicide detective and atheist-turned-Christian apologist J. Warner Wallace has researched the evidence drawn from many of the ancient church fathers' writings, and using forensic investigation skills, has established several chains of custody from the New Testament writers to the Church Council of Laodicea in A.D. 363 when the canon of 27 books was officially confirmed.[109]

He traces one of the strongest chains through the apostle Peter.[110] Peter's messages comprise the Gospel of Mark. Mark and Peter were close enough colleagues that in 1 Peter 5:13 Peter describes Mark as "my son."[111] Mark discipled and passed on the sacred writings to five men, one of whom was Justus, who passed them to Pantaenus, an "ex-Stoic philosopher who converted to Christianity."[112] Pantaenus taught Clement of Alexandria (ca. A.D. 150-215), who quoted or referred to all the New Testament books, except Philemon, James, 2 Peter, 2 John, and 3 John, which means he had received the list of accepted canonical books from his predecessors, 22 of the 27 later formally canonized. Clement taught the Egyptian church father Origen (A.D. 185-254), who wrote commentaries on virtually every biblical book and quoted from every New Testament book, confirming all 27.[113] Pamphilus defended the works of Origen after Origen was expelled from Alexandria under persecution, and Pamphilus also taught Eusebius of Caesarea (A.D. 263-339), a well-known church historian. Wallace concludes,

> This chain of scriptural custody, from Peter to Eusebius, brings us well into the period of time in which the Codex Sinaiticus was penned and to the doorstep of the Council of Laodicea. It is clear that the eyewitness accounts and writings of the apostles were collected, preserved, and transmitted from generation to generation during this span of time.[114]

We have examined reasons to believe that we can reconstruct the original New Testament writings with confidence beyond a reasonable doubt for the vast majority of the text. If the New Testament manuscripts are not accepted as reliable, all other copies of ancient writings must be dismissed, as well. For the New Testament boasts far more copies and far less of a time gap from the originals to the earliest copies than any other ancient writing. It also displays a tight chain of custody from the eyewitness era to the early church councils that confirmed the canon of the 27 books of the New Testament.

16

Were the New Testament Writers Who They Claimed to Be?

We have looked at the evidence supporting our claim that we can reconstruct with reasonable confidence what the originals said. Beyond the trustworthiness of the manuscripts, though, is another issue that must be addressed. Even if we can confidently reconstruct the original New Testament writings from the manuscripts we now have, we still haven't demonstrated that the writers of the originals were who they claimed to be, that they told the truth, or that their accounts were accurate. The first critical question is, Were the writers who they claimed to be? The New Testament writers claim to be eyewitnesses to the life of Jesus (or of the events for which they claim to be eyewitnesses), or contemporaries of the eyewitnesses who oversaw their writings.

A few years ago I attended a seminar at Queens University in Charlotte, North Carolina, hosting Richard Dawkins as speaker. Though the atheist scientist has no expertise in the area of New Testament textual criticism, that did not stop him from adamantly proclaiming that the New Testament writers were a bunch of "illiterate goat-herders." Laughter peppered the audience, with the exclusion, of course, of Christians in attendance.

Unlike Dawkins, agnostic New Testament scholar Bart Ehrman is well credentialed in the area of New Testament studies, and he agrees with Dawkins on this point, saying that "the disciples of Jesus were lower-class, illiterate, Aramaic-speaking peasants from Galilee. They could not read, let alone write. None of them wrote down what Jesus said."[115] Thus, they did not write anything. Rather, the Gospels were written "by highly literate, Greek-speaking Christians living 40–65 years after the death of Jesus."[116] While Ehrman asserts that we can't be sure who wrote the Gospels, he *is* sure the disciples of Jesus were illiterate peasants. He further concludes,

> These authors were not eyewitnesses. They lived in different countries from Jesus. They spoke a different language from Jesus. They did not have extensive written documentation from those who were eyewitnesses to Jesus because there was no documentation.[117]

In fact, he says, they never even claimed to be eyewitnesses. He is also quick to dismiss as alien to mainstream biblical scholarship the opposing view, insisting, "Let me stress: this is NOT a disputed point among critical scholars of the New Testament or ancient historians generally."[118] Of course, for Ehrman, the only legitimate scholarship is "higher criticism" of the Bible, which views the Bible as an error-ridden patchwork of documents. One would think based on Ehrman's comments that the only *real* scholars are the higher critics.

On the other hand, conservative evangelical Christian New Testament scholars such as Daniel Wallace, F.F. Bruce, Thomas Howe, Maurice Robinson, David Alan Black, Bruce Metzger (with whom Ehrman studied), and many others, who are as highly credentialed as Ehrman, believe that all of the New Testament writers lived during the first century A.D., and either walked personally with Jesus as apostles or were apostolic men: colleagues of the apostles, who wrote with their approval and oversight. For example, Luke was not an apostle; rather, he was Paul's physician and travelling companion. Mark was not an apostle; he was Peter's amanuensis (recorder) and his Gospel contains messages presented by Peter.

Ehrman and other higher critics ignore or discount the fact that the Jewish people as a whole were generally more literate than their surrounding neighbors, having memorized and studied large tracts of the Torah as children. Further, the professions of several of the writers required literacy. Luke was a physician, Mark was Peter's amanuensis (a person who serves as a scribe for someone, so he clearly was able to write), Matthew was a tax collector—which required meticulous record keeping and communication skills—and Paul was highly educated. So, whether through an amanuensis or by personal hand, the traditional New Testament writers were likely qualified and able to author their books.

Not all books contain the authors' names. Hebrews is anonymous and there are differences of opinion among the early church fathers as to authorship, but we need to remember that just because today we do not know the name of the author, this does not mean he was unknown *at the time*. Further, David Alan Black develops strong internal and external evidential arguments demonstrating striking commonalities between Hebrews and Paul's style and syntax in his other writings.[119] While 1-3 John did not contain the author's name, early on the letters were viewed as having the same author as John's Gospel.

The patristic witnesses, (another name for early church theologians or fathers who lived within the first few hundred years after Jesus' life), says Black, confirm that

> each of the four Gospels came into existence in response to the needs of the church at different moments during the lifetime of the original Twelve. This tradition is enshrined in the writings of early fathers of the church and was generally adopted by all the churches, east and west, down to the eighteenth century.[120]

He lists 14 patristic witnesses to the authenticity of the Gospels, of which we will only mention a few:

Matthew: One of the earliest church scholars, Bishop Papias (ca. 60-130), was quoted by ancient historian Eusebius (ca. 260-341), as saying regarding Matthew: "About Matthew this was said: So then Matthew composed the sayings . . . in a Hebrew style. . . ."[121] Irenaeus (ca. 130-200) was also quoted by Eusebius as confirming that Matthew "brought out a written gospel among the Jews in their own style."[122]

Mark: Papias confirmed that "Mark, having become the recorder . . . of Peter, indeed wrote accurately albeit not in order whatever he [Peter] remembered of the things either said or done by the Lord. . . . He had but one intention: not to leave out anything he had heard nor to falsify anything in them."[123] Papias confirmed that Mark passed on to disciples, himself included, "what had been proclaimed by Peter" (see Mark 3:16).[124] (Also Justin [ca. 100-165], Clement of Alexandria [ca. 150-215], Muratorian Fragment [second century], Jerome [ca. 345-420]).[125]

Luke: Irenaeus (ca. 130-200) was quoted by Eusebius as saying that "Luke, the follower of Paul, set forth in a book the gospel that was proclaimed by him."[126] (Also Muratorian Fragment [second century]).[127]

John: Irenaeus said that "later John the disciple of the Lord and the one who leaned against his chest, also put out a gospel while residing in Ephesus of Asia."[128] (Also Old Latin Prologue to Mark [rescension 2; second century]).[129]

In addition to the ones mentioned above, the following church fathers also confirmed that there were four Gospels that were written by the authors traditionally believed to have written them: Tertullian (ca. 160-225), Origen (ca. 185-254), Augustine (ca. 354-430).[130] The above comprise but a few of the citations of early church scholars, men committed to the Lord, who, by all accounts were men of integrity who followed in the footsteps of the apostles and their disciples, some of them claiming to know the apostles themselves. Consistently they record that there were four Gospels, all written by the persons whose names they bear.

What about evidence for the traditional authorship of other New Testament books? We will take a look at several:

Acts: *The Muratorian Fragment*, dated to ca. 170 is the oldest list of New Testament books, containing 22 of the 27 in its list. Eighty-five lines long, and difficult to read, the fragment was found in 1740,[131] and says the "acts of all the apostles were written in one book."[132] From the earliest times, Acts was viewed as the second book or second half of Luke's writing.

Internal evidence, that is, evidence in the words of the book itself, suggests that it was likely written before A.D. 62 since the death of three major leaders in the New Testament church—James the brother of Jesus (died A.D. 61), Peter, and Paul (died A.D. 62-68)—are not mentioned, while Stephen's and James' (the brother of John) deaths are mentioned. In fact, Paul was still imprisoned at the close of Acts.

Further, Acts is the only historical book in the New Testament, yet it does not mention the greatest historical event of the century for the Jews, the fall of Jerusalem in A.D. 70 (nor does any other New Testament book, for that matter). While not conclusive for early dating, it is significant since Luke, a meticulous historian by all accounts, would not have omitted this momentous event in the life of the Jewish people. Acts was written, then, after Luke, and before the deaths of Peter and Paul (ca. A.D. 62-68), as well as before the fall of Jerusalem (A.D. 70).

Epistles and Revelation: Daniel Wallace and Bart Ehrman, though one is a believer and one a skeptic, both agree that there is no question about Paul's authorship of 1 Corinthians.[133] Further, there is a general consensus that the book was written by A.D. 56, based on the internal evidence, such as the chronology of events that suggest the book was written somewhere in the middle of Paul's three-year tenure in Ephesus, and thus, about A.D. 54.[134] They also both confirm that "virtually all scholars" also agree that Romans, 2 Corinthians, Galatians, Philippians, 1 Thessalonians, and Philemon are genuine Pauline letters.[135]

What does *The Muratorian Fragment* say about the epistles and John's Revelation?

As for the Epistles of Paul, they themselves make clear to those desiring to understand, which ones [they are], from what place, or for what reason they were sent. First of all, to the Corinthians, prohibiting their heretical schisms; next, to the Galatians, against circumcision; then to the Romans. He wrote at length, explaining the order (or, plan) of the Scriptures, and also that Christ is their principle (or, main theme). It is necessary for us to discuss these one by one, since the blessed apostle Paul himself, following the example of his predecessor John, writes by name to only seven churches in the following sequence: To the Corinthians first, to the Ephesians second, to the Philippians third, to the Colossians fourth, to the Galatians fifth, to the Thessalonians sixth, to the Romans seventh. It is true that he writes once more to the Corinthians and to the Thessalonians for the sake of admonition, yet it is clearly recognizable that there is one Church spread throughout the whole extent of the earth. For John also in the Apocalypse, though he writes to seven churches, nevertheless speaks to all. [Paul also wrote] out of affection and love one to Philemon, one to Titus, and two to Timothy; and these are held sacred. . . . Moreover, the epistle of Jude and two of the above-mentioned (or, bearing the name of) John are counted.[136]

The writer notes that there was also a book known as *The Apocalypse of Peter.* He says that it was not permitted to be read in some of the churches, indicating the distinctions already being made between writings to be considered divinely inspired and those that were of doubtful origin, written after the apostolic era, or to be treated as suitable for devotional reading but not as sacred.

By the beginning of the third century A.D. both Irenaeus and Origin's lists of books included all but Hebrews (Origen included Hebrews), 2 Peter, 2 and 3 John, James and Jude, and by the mid-fourth century Athanasius listed all 27 books.

Biblical scholar F.F. Bruce then says that "the first ecclesiastical councils to classify the canonical books were both held in North Africa — at Hippo Regius in 393 and at Carthage in 397 — but what these councils did was not to impose something new upon the Christian communities but to codify what was already the general practice of those communities."[137] Thus, the councils affirmed what the churches already held to be true about the books comprising those inspired by God. They did not *make* the books canonical; they discovered and affirmed those *already recognized* as canonical.

But did forgeries or other extraneous books make their way into our New Testament? As J. Warner Wallace has shown, the apostles had disciples who had disciples who had disciples who had disciples. Thus, there is strong evidence that the sacred texts were passed across each generation intact. The implications of this are not only that the canon (the list of sacred books) is secure, but also that the books likely could not have been written later or by forgers and made their way into the churches as revered texts.

There were certainly forgeries. *The Muratorian Fragment* actually mentions them and how they were dealt with: "There is currently also [an epistle] to the Laodiceans, [and] another to the Alexandrians, [both] forged in Paul's name to [further] the heresy of Marcion, and several others which cannot be received . . . for it is not fitting that gall be mixed with honey."[138] As the writer notes, there is no reason to think that the churches actually adopted forged writings as genuine, replicating and distributing them to the extent that they made their way into what we now believe is the inspired New Testament canon.

17

Were the New Testament Writers Trustworthy? The Internal Evidence

According to skeptic Ehrman, the Gospels are filled with errors and contradictions. "One of the reasons the Gospel narratives are filled with so many discrepancies and contradictions is that the authors were not able to base their accounts on substantial numbers of records made by people who had accompanied Jesus at the time."[139]

Charles Darwin was also convinced of the New Testament writers ineptitude:

> The Gospels cannot be proved to have been written simultaneously with the events,—that they differ in many important details, far too important, as it seemed to me, to be admitted as the usual inaccuracies of eye-witnesses;— by such reflections as these, which I give not as having the least novelty or value, but as they influenced me, I gradually came to disbelieve in Christianity as a divine revelation. The fact that many false religions have spread over large portions of the earth like wild-fire had some weight with me.[140]

We almost feel sorry for the bumbling New Testament writers of Ehrman's and Darwin's view. But were they really bumbling after all? The internal evidence does not comport with their assertions.

New Testament Writers Clarified Their Sources

The apostle **John**, who wrote five New Testament books, affirmed that he personally knew Jesus Christ (1 John 1:1-4). **Peter** wrote two books and supervised Mark's Gospel in which Peter's remembrances of the Lord's words and deeds were recorded. The apostle **Paul**, whose life was transformed on the road to Damascus when he met Christ, wrote 13 New Testament letters, and described Christ's appearing to him "as to one untimely born" (1 Cor. 15:8). He also verified that he received direct revelation of the gospel from Jesus Christ: "For I did not receive it from any man, nor was I taught it, but I received it through a revelation of Jesus Christ" (Gal. 1:12-16). He says that he later conferred with Peter and James, the brother of Christ.

Luke, on the other hand, the author of Luke and Acts, and the writer who contributed the greatest number of words to the New Testament, clarified that his was a journalistic endeavor in which he interviewed eyewitnesses. At the opening his Gospel, he said that he recorded carefully what he had been told. Just as we accept as legitimate a journalist's account in which the eyewitnesses are interviewed and the journalist records what she is told by them, we have good reason to trust Luke's method of interview and recording. The very fact that Luke clarified that he was not a personal eyewitness of Christ strengthens the likelihood he told the truth.

Luke was an eyewitness, however, to many of the events in Acts, in which he says "we," confirming that he was present with Paul on many occasions. Paul was able to supervise and confirm Luke's writings as accurate.

As mentioned, we are not given the name of the writer of **Hebrews.** However, it does not follow that because we don't know his name, he was therefore not known at the time of his writing. He claimed that the Lord declared the gospel message and those who walked with Him and heard Him during His life also verified the message, sharing it with the next generation of believers: "How shall we escape if we neglect such a great salvation? It was declared at first by the Lord, and it was attested to us by those who heard" (Heb. 2:3).

Specificity of the New Testament Writers' Details Invited Verification

If a person wants to fool others into thinking he was present at a certain event at a specific location, the way to do this is *not* by including too many details. Yet this is just what we see in the narratives written by the New Testament authors. In fact, they often included details so specific that they could have been easily falsified if the claims were not true.

A case in point is biblical writer **Luke**, who F.F. Bruce says was from Antioch of Syria. Luke was a meticulous historian, discussing the roles of numerous historical figures in the events of Christ's life and ministry. He refers to Quirinius, Pilate, Sergius Paullus, Gallio, Felix, Festus, Herod the Great, Herod Antipas, Herod Agrippa I and II, Bernice, Drusilla, Annas, Caiaphas, Ananias, and Gamaliel. Bruce observes the significance of Luke's references to so many prominent political and religious leaders.

> A writer who thus relates his story to the wider context of world history is courting trouble if he is not careful; he affords his critical readers so many opportunities for testing his accuracy. Luke takes this risk and stands the test admirably. One of the most remarkable tokens of his accuracy is his sure familiarity with the proper titles of all the notable persons who are mentioned in his pages.[141]

In his book of Acts Luke traced Peter and Paul's ministries in the growth of the early church and the spread of the gospel throughout the world. Ehrman claims that the writer of Acts "was almost certainly not a companion of Paul's," because "he seems to be far too poorly informed about Paul's theology and missionary activities to have been someone with firsthand knowledge."[142] This is at odds with the assessment of Scottish archaeologist and New Testament scholar, Sir William Ramsay (1851-1939), who found after years of research in Asia Minor, evidence for just the opposite: "The characterisation of Paul in Acts is so detailed and individualised as to prove the author's personal acquaintance."[143] Ramsay came to his conclusion, not due to any bias in favor of Christianity. By his own confession he originally set out to disprove the authenticity of Luke's writings, but the evidence forced him to change his mind:

I may fairly claim to have entered on this investigation without any prejudice in favour of the conclusion which I shall now attempt to justify to the reader. On the contrary, I began with a mind unfavourable to it. . . . It did not lie then in my line of life to investigate the subject minutely; but more recently I found myself often brought in contact with the book of Acts as an authority for the topography, antiquities, and society of Asia Minor. It was gradually borne in upon me that in various details the narrative showed marvellous truth.[144]

Luke has not been without his critics. Higher critics—liberal scholars who argue that the New Testament is filled with errors—argue that he made errors in his narratives. One supposed error often cited is his claim in Luke 2:1-7 that Jesus was born during the time that a census was ordered by Quirinius, governor of Syria:

In those days a decree went out from Caesar Augustus that all the world should be registered. This was the first registration when Quirinius was governor of Syria. And all went to be registered, each to his own town. And Joseph also went up from Galilee, from the town of Nazareth, to Judea, to the city of David, which is called Bethlehem, because he was of the house and lineage of David, to be registered with Mary, his betrothed, who was with child. And while they were there, the time came for her to give birth. And she gave birth to her firstborn son and wrapped him in swaddling cloths and laid him in a manger, because there was no place for them in the inn.

The problem is that Jesus was born while King Herod was still alive, but Quirinius wasn't governor of Syria until several years after Herod's death. What are we to make of this apparent discrepancy? Princeton scholar John D. Davis insists that critics should not be so quick to dismiss Luke's assertions out-of-hand as error, given the fact that "Luke shows himself well informed on historical matters and his accuracy has been vindicated in many other instances."[145]

Luke clarified that this was the "first" registration, or census, which gives us a hint that the census to which he referred was not to be confused with a later census taken under his governorship, and that Luke was quite aware of (Acts 5:37). The discovery of a first-century Roman epitaph, the *titulus Tibertinus* in Tivoli, Italy, in 1764, mentions a leader who served as legate twice.[146] While there is still debate about the identity of the unnamed official and the dating of the first tenure of service, several Roman historians and archaeologists, including William Ramsay, argue that the inscription can only refer to Quirinius, and that the dating of the delegated official role would match the dating of Luke's timing of Christ's birth.[147] Given the fact that Luke was meticulous in dealing with numerous other facts, as Ramsay as shown, we can show him the courtesy of trusting him on the events surrounding Christ's birth, as well.

A couple of other examples will suffice to support the argument that the New Testament writers included specific details that demonstrate their concern for accuracy. Because these details, if untrue, can be falsified easily, their inclusion is helpful in affirming the reliability of the author.

Paul, for example, in 1 Corinthians 15:5-8, records the appearances of Christ after His resurrection, saying that

> he appeared to Cephas, then to the twelve. Then he appeared to more than five hundred brothers at one time, most of whom are still alive, though some have fallen asleep. Then he appeared to James, then to all the apostles. Last of all, as to one untimely born, he appeared also to me.

Paul specifically identified 500 people before whom Christ appeared alive. He added that most of the 500 were still living, opening the door to anyone who sought to verify his claims.

When called to give a defense, Paul stood before Agrippa and Festus and recounted his conversion experience on the Damascus road. When Festus responded that Paul was out of his mind, Paul said he was not. He was speaking rationally, he asserted, adding, "For the king knows about these things, and to him I speak boldly. For I am persuaded that none of these things has escaped his notice, for this has not been done in a corner" (Acts 26:26).

The apostle **John**'s Gospel has come under attack numerous times through the years. New Testament professor Craig Blomberg, though, argues that many characteristics of John's Gospel, rather,

> support a global verdict of historicity. These include the many points of "interlocking" with the Synoptics—places where either the Johannine or the Synoptic tradition contains puzzling

information that is only explained by information in the other tradition. Archaeological and topographical studies have confirmed John's consistent accuracy concerning the geography of Palestine overall as well as specific sites.[148]

One example from John 5:2-9 will give us insight to John's concern with accuracy and specificity in details: "Now there was in Jerusalem by the Sheep Gate a pool, in Aramaic called Bethesda, which has five roofed colonnades" (v. 2). Here by the pool that was believed to have medicinal healing powers lay the blind, lame, and paralyzed hoping for healing when the waters "stirred up." Among them was a man who had been an invalid for 38 years. Jesus asked him if he wanted to be healed. Of course, he did, but someone always got in the waters at the right time ahead of him. Jesus simply told him to get up and walk. The healing was instantaneous.

John's specific and odd description of a pool with five colonnades, suggesting five sides, rather than the normal four, invited scrutiny and criticism. When in the late 1800s the pool was discovered, says Paul Anderson, critics had to eat their words:

> The discovery of two pools, just outside the Sheep Gate (cf. Jn 5:2) in Jerusalem, which appear to have been by five porticos—porches sheltering the four-sided circumference of the pools, with a fifth roof sheltering the area between the pools. Interestingly enough, until archaeologists began excavating this site, it was assumed that a five-portico pool must have been a Johannine fabrication—perhaps a theologized reference to the five books of Moses. With the discovery, however, of a central roof-structure supported by 12 columns, and one on each of the four outer sides of the pool complex, the Johannine rendering is entirely accurate from an archaeological and historical standpoint. It was not a "fabricated" detail. Even the name of the pool, Bethzatha (not to be confused with Bethsaida, the home of Andrew and Peter as some manuscripts have), is corroborated by the reference in the Copper Scroll of Qumran (Cave 3, col. 11) to a pool in Jerusalem called Beth Eshdathayin (meaning "the place of the twin pools" . . .). In these and other ways, the scene described in Jn 15 is impressively corroborated by recent archaeological discoveries.[149]

Numerous other examples of verification of John's claims could be given, if space permitted. But the point is, that John, along with the two other writers, Luke and Paul, who wrote the bulk of the New Testament, were concerned with accuracy, were meticulous in their description of people, places, and events, and invited scrutiny of their assertions by giving specific details that could easily be verified or falsified by examination.

New Testament Writers Exhibited Honorable Character Traits

Ehrman criticizes Matthew, accusing him of falsifying his narrative about Christ in his Gospel. "Just because everyone else changed and made up stories, does that mean Matthew is accurate when he does so? That's kind of like saying that I haven't broken the law when I got a speeding ticket because everyone goes over the speed limit."[150] Evangelical scholars, on the other hand, argue that the writers were people of integrity by all accounts, and though they were flawed humans as revealed by their own writings, they were not given to flights of imagination, coercion, or manipulation to gain followers.

No Collusion; No Contradictions

Liberal scholars would have us think that where the Gospel writers agree on events and sayings in the life of Jesus that they colluded to sync their made-up stories, like two criminal suspects do when left together in an interrogation room for 10 minutes. On the other hand, they argue that where there are divergent details, they are contradictory. On closer examination, however, we find that the majority of apparent contradictions can easily be resolved, and that plausible interpretations may be applicable. Further, divergent details demonstrate that the eyewitnesses were telling the facts as they saw them, rather than colluding to contrive a false story.

To illustrate how apparent contradictions can often be resolved, I often shared with my high school students a real-life scenario. I, Tricia, spoke at a women's conference, along with another woman named Patty. Imagine I had two friends who came to the conference, both journalists for different publications who were writing articles about the event. Jonie wrote that Tricia spoke first and then Patty. Tamisha wrote that Patty spoke first and then Tricia. When I asked my students if both writers could be telling the truth, most responded that one of them was wrong. A few astute students realized that there is a scenario in which both could be accurately recording what they saw. The fact is that Patty spoke first, then I spoke in the early afternoon, then Patty spoke again after me. Tamisha came the whole day to the conference, and so she saw Patty speak first, then me. Jonie didn't arrive at the conference until late in the morning after Patty had already finished speaking the first time, so she first heard me speak, then heard Patty's late afternoon session.

Similarly, the Gospel writers recorded different details about the same events. But different details are not necessarily contradictory details. Here are a couple of commonly cited apparent contradictions that can be resolved instead of resorting to skepticism about the historical reliability of the documents.

Matthew records that there was one angel at Jesus' resurrection tomb, while John speaks of two. How could both be correct? Christian philosopher and apologist Norman Geisler explains:

> An eyewitness of Jesus' tomb standing at one place may have seen only one angel (Matt. 28:5), namely, the one angel who was at the head of corpse, but another eyewitness standing farther into the tomb was able to see both of them (Jn. 20:12). To be sure, the snap shots are from different angles and reveal different perspectives, but they are still accurate pictures of what Jesus actually said and did and what the witnesses saw. They are not interpretive creations.[151]

Matthew and Luke record apparently contradictory accounts of Judas' death. Matthew 27:5 says Judas died by hanging himself, whereas Luke says in Acts 1:18 that Judas fell headlong and his inner parts burst out. How could both be correct? Actually, very easily. Judas hanged himself. The body swelled and burst open as bodies do when they decompose. Both accounts can be reconciled with a reasonable explanation that does not require imaginative leaps.

The Gospel writers often use different wording to describe the Lord's words in certain scenes. As Geisler notes, Peter's confession is worded somewhat differently in the Gospels. But, as he points out, "While we do not in most cases have the exact words of Jesus (*ipsissima verba*), there is good reason to believe that we do have the true meaning of them (*ipsissima vox*)."[152]

Humility; Not Arrogance

James, the half-brother of Jesus, introduced himself in his epistle as "James, a servant of God, and of the Lord Jesus Christ" (James 1:1). Not a word did he say about his relationship to Jesus. Significant for the trustworthiness of James' eyewitness account is the fact that he did not believe in Jesus during His ministry on earth (see John 7:1-5). The resurrection convinced him, and according to church history, he became a beloved and fervent leader of the Jerusalem church.

It is also very possible that Jude, who wrote one epistle, was the half-brother of Jesus, as well. We cannot be certain, but his referencing himself as half-brother of James, may very well have also been an effort at modesty.

Paul was a bold preacher of the gospel. Though he affirmed that he was an apostle, he described himself as "the least of the apostles, unworthy to be called an apostle, because I persecuted the church of God" (1 Cor. 15:9). As for Luke, Ramsay says,

> It is rare to find a narrative so simple and so little forced as that of Acts. It is a mere uncoloured recital of the important facts in the briefest possible terms. The narrator's individuality and his personal feelings and preferences are almost wholly suppressed. He is entirely absorbed in his work; and he writes with the single aim to state the facts as he has learned them.[153]

The writers exhibited humility, even about their failures.

> The mother of the sons of Zebedee came up to him with her sons, and kneeling before him she asked him for something. And he said to her, "What do you want?" She said to him, "Say that these two sons of mine are to sit, one at your right hand and one at your left, in your kingdom" (Matt. 20:20-21).

James and John have their mother ask for favored positions at the Lord's right and left hands in the coming kingdom. We might conclude that their characters were flawed. They were. But the most character revealing aspect of this story is that this account of embarrassing selfishness was not excised when the apostles could easily have squelched it.

Peter's story of denial is included in Mark's Gospel (Mark 14:66-72). Given the fact that Mark was his amanuensis, or recorder, Peter had to have given his approval for publication of this sordid event, an experience that clearly revealed Peter's over-confidence and cowardice. But, it is not merely the sin that reveals the character, but one's response to it. Peter grieved over his failure and was restored to the Lord, eventually standing courageously in the face of great opposition and preaching the Word with boldness. This fact reminds us that when we fail, our failure is not the final word on our character.

Comparing what we know of the apostles with what we know about the Latter Day Saints church founder Joseph Smith is an exercise in contrast. In the Prologue of his book, *In Sacred Loneliness,* Todd Compton says, "I have identified thirty-three well-documented wives of Joseph Smith," adding that his count may be on the low side as compared with others' research findings.[154] Solely based on this piece of evidence, many (I think, rightfully) would call him a lust-driven, promiscuous man, and a father who abandoned his own children, since there is no way he could adequately father or provide for children of that many wives.

Smith's lust was surpassed only by his arrogance:

> I am the only man that has ever been able to keep a whole church together since the days of Adam. A large majority of the whole have stood by me. Neither Paul, John, Peter, nor Jesus ever did it. I boast that no man ever did such a work as I. The followers of Jesus ran away from Him; but the Latter-day Saints never ran away from me yet.[155]

How different the apostle Paul and Joseph Smith look through the lens of humility.

Uncompromising; Not Pandering

If you want to sell a religion, telling people that they must love their enemies (Matt. 5:44), be willing to abandon all that is precious to them to follow God (Matt. 19:24), and that if they even look at a woman lustfully they have already committed adultery in their hearts (Matt. 5:28), is not the way to win them over. Further, those who wished to follow Christ must come to Him recognizing that they were hopeless, dirty sinners who stood without excuse before a Holy God. And, oh, by the way, they were going to suffer. Welcome to Christianity.

The New Testament writers recognized that Christ's demands were exclusive, all-encompassing, and required self-denial. Yet, they fearlessly presented the message and promised that following Christ would be costly, though worth every sacrifice.

Faithful; Not Flinching

As we've already mentioned, the New Testament evidence shows that the disciples did indeed flinch in the hours before Jesus' crucifixion. They all abandoned the Lord, at least temporarily, except John, who hovered near. But as we have talked about as well, the Gospel writers courageously wrote about (and published for the churches to read), descriptions of their own failures, cast in the light of Christ's love.

Ultimately, though, when their lives were on the line, history records that all but John, who died a natural death but suffered in exile, willingly embraced a martyr's death (see Acts 14:19-22). While their faithfulness to the point of death does not prove that their claims were true, it demonstrates that they sincerely believed their claims were true, and thus, they were not charlatans or power-mongers.

18

Were the New Testament Writers Trustworthy? The External Evidence

Not only did the eyewitnesses sincerely believe the gospel message of Jesus Christ and confirm His words, deeds, death, and resurrection, early church scholars and historians confirm a narrative consistent with the New Testament account. J. W. Wallace observes that simply on the basis of the non-biblical writings of three disciples of the eyewitnesses—Ignatius of Antioch, Polycarp of Smyrna, and Clement of Rome—we have corroborating evidence of many New Testament claims about Jesus Christ. Just a few include that "He was the only begotten Son of God, born of the virgin Mary . . . Baptized by John the Baptist, . . . spoke the words of God, . . . and [was] ultimately executed on the cross."[156] These writers "made no conscious effort to record the details of Jesus's life" and yet they clearly confirm numerous details that they could only have received from the eyewitnesses and which are also recorded in the New Testament Gospels.[157]

But external to the Christian community, is there historical information provided by ancient historians or other writers that give us a picture of Jesus Christ? Historical records show that there are.

Pagan Ancient Writers Confirm New Testament Benchmarks of Christ's Life

In addition to the verification of the main events of Jesus' life by ancient Christian writers, non-Christian writers who lived shortly after the time of Christ, some apathetic about Christianity and others openly hostile, also recorded a similar narrative of the core facts about Jesus' life and about His followers. F.F. Bruce, in his book, *The New Testament Documents: Are They Reliable?*, has identified comments about Jesus found in writings including the Jewish Talmud, ancient Jewish historian Josephus, Tacitus, Pliny the Younger, Emperor Trajan, Phlegon, Thallus, and Greek writer Lucian. These comments affirm the benchmarks of the New Testament narrative, and we will examine several examples as presented by Bruce.

Josephus ca. A.D. 37-100

The Jewish historian Josephus (A.D. 37-100) was the main Jewish historian of first-century A.D. He had a colorful career, to say the least. A commander in the Jewish revolt against the Romans, the story goes that he opted to surrender to them after making a suicide pact in which all but one other soldier died. Needless to say, he was not a popular man among his people, who viewed him as a traitor.[158]

Nevertheless, we have him to thank for voluminous works on Jewish history. His writings, which, according to experts, show clear evidence of independence from the biblical writers, confirm the existence of numerous first-century figures who played significant roles in the narrative about Jesus' and Paul's lives. Officials such as Augustus, Tiberius, Claudius, Nero, Quirinius, Pilate, Felix, and Festus; Jewish high priests Annas and Caiaphas; as well as Pharisees and Sadducees religious sects; all make their appearances in Josephus's writings. He recorded the famine during the time of Claudius, mentioned by Luke in Acts 11:28. He also talked about John the Baptist, saying that Herod killed him "though he was a good man,"[159] and spoke of John's practice of baptism. Regarding Jesus, the traditional passage reads as follows:

> And there arose about this time Jesus, a wise man, if indeed we should call him a man; for he was a doer of marvelous deeds, a teacher of men who receive the truth with pleasure. He led away many Jews, and also many of

the Greeks. This man was the Christ. And when Pilate had condemned him to the cross on his impeachment by the chief men among us, those who had loved him at first did not cease; for he appeared to them on the third day alive again, the divine prophets having spoken these and thousands of other wonderful things about him: and even now the tribe of Christians, so named after him, has not yet died out.[160]

Given the fact that church father Origen said Josephus was not a believer in Christ, many have questioned whether this wording is original to Josephus. Bruce speculates that the sections that speak glowingly of the Lord may have been written sarcastically. It should be said, though, when we respond to skeptics who argue that the passage was not original with Josephus, that even some liberal critical scholars accept the original form.

Nevertheless, a common amended form of the quote that eliminates suspected later Christian changes still contains significant information verifying the same narrative that Gospel writers affirmed regarding Christ's life, as well as Jewish leaders' view of Him. The amended form affirms that Jesus was called a "wise man," a "doer of marvelous deeds, a teacher," who "led away many Jews . . . and Greeks," was called "Christ," was condemned by Pilate to the cross on the basis of accusations by the Jewish leaders, had faithful followers who said that he "appeared to them, as they said, on the third day alive again, the divine prophets having spoken these and thousands of other wonderful things about him," and that the Christian sect still existed at the time of Josephus.[161] Thus, the main points about Jesus' life are preserved.

Thallus A.D. 52

A freedman under Tiberius, Thallus recorded a history of Greece from the time of the Trojan War up to his present day. Thallus lived during the era of the eyewitnesses in the first century, but, not surprisingly, we do not have his original writings. Fortunately, about A.D. 221 a Christian writer named Julius Africanus affirmed that Thallus described the unique darkness during Christ's crucifixion: "Thallus . . . explains away the darkness as an eclipse of the sun—unreasonably, as it seems to me (unreasonably, of course because a solar eclipse could not take place at the time of the full moon, and it was at the season of the Paschal full moon that Christ died)."[162]

Africanus evaluated Thallus' comment about the pervasive darkness that covered the land during Christ's crucifixion. Though Thallus suggested it was due to a solar eclipse, Africanus asserted that it was not the time for a solar eclipse and therefore, could not be explained by natural causes. Thallus' assertion is valuable since, as Africanus notes, Thallus provides a pagan attestation of the events surrounding Christ's death.

Tacitus A.D. 109

The terrible fate of Christians under the rule of Nero (A.D. 54-68), said the Roman historian, Tacitus, came about as a result of Nero trying to squelch rumors that he himself started the great fire of Rome in A.D. 64.

Nero substituted as culprits, and punished with the utmost refinement of cruelty, a class of men . . . whom the crowd styled Christians. Christus, from whom they got their name, had been executed by sentence of the procurator Pontius Pilate when Tiberius was emperor.[163]

It was under the scourge of Nero's rule that both Peter and Paul were executed.

Pliny the Younger A.D. 112

Writing Emperor Trajan, the governor of Bithynia, Pliny, sought advice on how to handle the annoying sect of fanatics called Christians. Under torture, he said, some had confessed that "they were in the habit of meeting on a certain fixed day before it was light, when they sang an anthem to Christ as God, and bound themselves by a solemn oath . . . not to commit any wicked deed."[164]

Pliny had no vested interest in the Christian story; to him Christians were a fly in the ointment. Nevertheless, by his own words, the Christian sect flourished during the time of Nero, meeting before dawn to worship. And the centerpiece of their worship was Jesus Christ, whom they worshipped as God.

Justin Martyr ca. A.D. 150

Defending Christianity to the emperor, Christian Justin Martyr advised him to consult Pilate's official report to verify the means of Christ's death. Evidently, Pilate's records, (a pagan source), said Justin, would confirm "nails that were fixed in His hands and His feet on the cross; and after He was crucified, those who crucified Him cast lots for His garments, and divided them among themselves." Later, Martyr also referred to the miracles of Christ.[165]

What inferences can we draw from the above ancient sources dating back to the first century A.D.? Jesus Christ lived early in the first century, He had a brother named James, He was known as a wonder worker and teacher, He was called Christ—the Anointed One—the Messiah that some believed had been prophesied in the *TaNaKh* (the Jewish Old Testament), He had a large following of both Jews and Gentiles, which the Jewish leaders resented. He was prosecuted and condemned to death by procurator Pilate at the time of Passover, in response to the accusations of Jewish leaders. He was crucified with His hands and feet nailed to a cross, and during His crucifixion, a pervasive and unusual darkness blanketed the land, one that could not be explained by an eclipse. Soldiers gambled for His garments while He hung on the cross. His followers claimed that He arose from the dead and appeared to them after His resurrection. After Christ's death and resurrection, the Christian sect flourished and continued their distinctive religion, worshipping Christ as God. They suffered excruciating persecution and torture at the hands of Nero. Christ's followers covenanted together to live holy lives.

What may we conclude? Bruce concludes that "the historicity of Christ is as axiomatic for an unbiased historian as the historicity of Julius Caesar."[166] We can trace the same story through ancient historical writings as we do through the Gospels. Years after His death people were still talking about the events surrounding Christ that shook the nation, including His resurrection. Jesus Christ's impact not only lived after him, but also sparked a movement that continues to this day.

Some ask, Why not more writings about Christ? Bruce says the reason is simple. Christianity in its first 100 years was considered "an obscure, disreputable, vulgar oriental superstition."[167] But it should also be noted that more is written in ancient history about Jesus Christ than about many of the Caesars and other prominent figures of history. Palestine, the backwaters of the Roman Empire, would have gone largely unnoticed had not the Jews revolted and Jesus Christ made His appearance on the scene. If the overarching narrative of Christ's life is rejected, then we must also purge history books of many of the prominent figures of ancient history.

Archaeology Corroborates New Testament Claims

When I travelled to Israel in May 2016 what struck me as most significant was the wealth of historical information accessible not just horizontally *across* the land but also vertically *beneath* virtually every rock, church or lake bed. Israel's history is as deep as it is wide, so to speak. I'd like to share with you just a few of the archaeological discoveries (out of thousands) that strengthen my own faith by confirming the historical facts that serve as the geographical and cultural context for the Gospel narratives.

When we talk about archaeological finds, we need to be careful not to claim that these discoveries *prove* the New Testament is true. Generally speaking, the role of archaeology is to *corroborate* New Testament claims by providing supporting evidence about people, places, and events. If, for instance, Luke said that a census occurred by a governor named Quirinius, during which time Mary and Joseph traveled to Bethlehem, and archaeological discoveries provided evidence that Quirinius was not governor at that time, we would have to research further to decide how the discrepancy occurred. In fact, as we have discussed, this is an actual apparent discrepancy that has several legitimate resolution possibilities.

On the other hand, if we found an inscription that included Pilate's name and date, saying he was prefect of Judea, while that would not confirm the New Testament narrative regarding his presiding over Jesus' crucifixion as the Gospels record, it would provide corroborative evidence for specific assertions about Pilate's existence in that office at that time in Judea.

The Pilate Inscription

Early in our Israel trip we visited Caesarea Maritima, nestled in the Plain of Sharon, one of the most fertile places in the world. Herod built there a massive artificial harbor capable of holding 300 ships and an amphitheater with seating for 3,500 people where people watched play performances. He also constructed a hippodrome for horse races, and later, Christians were martyred there.[168]

As I sat in the reconstructed seats of the gargantuan amphitheater listening to our guide, I pondered the machinations that went on in this place some 2,000 years ago. Herod's power and skill were garishly obvious. He obviously believed, "Go big or go home." Remains of his palace still jut out into the Mediterranean Sea, hinting at the opulence that must have been. But I was interested in the site for another reason.

In June 1961 Italian archaeologists excavated an ancient Roman amphitheater, unearthing a piece of limestone that was inscribed with a dedication to Tiberius Caesar from "Pontius Pilate, Prefect of Judea." The Pilate Inscription, as it is called, provides historical extra-biblical evidence confirming that Pilate was prefect of Judea during the time that Christ was interrogated and crucified.

What questions does this artifact answer?

*Did the Pilate purported by the Gospels to have presided over the indictment of Christ really exist?
*Did he exist during the time the New Testament writers say that Jesus was tried and crucified?
*Was he in the geographical location that New Testament writers asserted?
*Was he serving in the official role that the writers affirmed?

The answer is, Yes.

The Pool of Siloam

Sitting at the excavation site of the Pool of Siloam we read John chapter nine, the apostle's account of Jesus' healing the blind man. It was common for beggars to sit on the southern steps leading to the Temple. As the Savior passed by, John says, He saw the blind man, made a daub of mud with spit and dirt, smeared it on the man's eyes, and told him to go wash in the Pool of Siloam. The exact location of the pool as it was in the time of Christ had been a mystery until June 2004, when, during the repair of water pipes, archaeologists observed remains of ancient steps, which were identified as those of the first-century pool.[169]

What questions does this archaeological discovery answer?

*Was John correct in saying that the Pool of Siloam existed in the time of Christ?
*Was it in the proximity of the temple location where it was customary for the crippled, blind, and beggars to sit, making reasonable Christ's command to "go wash" in the pool?

The answer is, Yes.

First Century Crucifixion Victim

The Jews in ancient history did not commonly practice crucifixion. Ancient Greek historian Herodotus (c. 484–425 BC) suggested that the Persians originated the gruesome practice, speaking of one Persian leader who practiced it, saying: "He took the Magi who interpreted dreams, who had persuaded him to let Cyrus go free, and impaled them."[170]

If the Persians invented crucifixion, the Romans perfected it. Archaeologist Vassilios Tzaferas says that "from ancient literary sources we know that tens of thousands of people were crucified in the Roman Empire. In Palestine alone, the figure ran into the thousands. Yet until 1968 not a single victim of this horrifying method of execution had been uncovered archaeologically."[171] Then, during post-Six Day War construction projects, the remains of a crucifixion victim literally turned up, including an ankle bone still attached to a tiny piece of wood.[172]

Questions that this artifact answers include the following:

*Were accounts of crucifixion, both in ancient pagan writings and in the Gospels grounded in a practice that was actually practiced in first century Judea?
*Were victims often nailed through the feet or ankles?
*Were these victims impaled on wooden edifices?

The answer is, Yes.

Nazareth

The Gospels describe Nazareth as the village in which Jesus grew up. When he began His public ministry, He returned there to the synagogue. He read from chapter 61 of the Isaiah scroll, asserting that He himself fulfilled the messianic prophecy. The religious leaders were so angered that they attempted to throw him from the cliff at the village's edge (Luke 4:16-30), but He escaped.

During our visit to Nazareth it was hard to miss The Church of the Annunciation dwarfing the landscape. The site is historically believed to be the site where Mary received her message from the angel Gabriel that she was to give birth to Messiah. In December 2009, adjacent to the Church of Annunciation, a first-century house was discovered. It was comprised of two rooms, a courtyard, and a water-collecting cistern.[173]

What questions does this discovery answer?

*Did a village called Nazareth exist in the Galilee area in the time of Christ?
*Was it a stable village in which people lived?
*Did the villagers build homes and seek a reliable water supply as evidence of long-term dwelling?

The answer is, Yes.

Caiaphas' Bones

In August 1992, the New York Times reported the discovery of the bones of Caiaphas, high priest A.D. 18-36, and interrogator of Christ according to Gospel writers (Matt. 27:57-66, Mark 14:53-65, and John 18:19-24). Exquisitely ornate, the box revealed a common practice of the Jews: digging up the bones of those buried a year prior, and placing them in an ossuary.[174]

While in Israel we visited the Israel Museum where the ossuary is on display. The bones have been removed from the ossuary and reburied on the Mount of Olives.

Questions that this discovery helps to answer:

*Did Caiaphas live during the early first century A.D.?
*Do the accoutrements of the ossuary suggest that it holds the bones of someone of prominence?
*Is it likely that it was the same Caiaphas whom Gospel writers claim interrogated Christ?

The answer is, Yes.

Hundreds more archaeological discoveries could be cited that corroborate the New Testament assertions about the culture, the geography, and the socio-political environment in which Jesus was born, grew up, ministered, died, and arose. Numerous ancient historians and officials of the Greco-Roman Empire confirmed the overarching narrative that the New Testament records. Based on the evidential support, we can reasonably conclude that the New Testament is reliable in what it says Jesus did and said, and in its claims regarding the earliest stages, growth, and expansion of the early church.

19

Did Jesus and His Disciples Believe He Was God?

Many people think that Jesus never claimed to be God in the flesh, but the New Testament shows that He clearly did. While His claiming to be God does not prove He is God, if He did not claim to be God there is no reason we should elevate Him to that status. This is exactly the argument that Jehovah's Witnesses make, so we should be ready to offer evidence that the New Testament writers verified that Jesus claimed to be God in asserting that He had the same character, eternality, power, and authority over nature, sickness, sin, and death as the Father.

Jesus Claimed to Be the Old Testament "I Am"

One of the strongest evidences of Jesus' claim to deity comes from a comparison of two passages: Exodus 3:14 and John 8:58-59. In Exodus 3:14 God speaks to Moses, instructing him to go to the Israelites, telling them that he was God's spokesman, and promising that God would free them from bondage through his leadership. Moses was naturally reluctant. "If I come to the people of Israel and say to them, 'The God of your fathers has sent me to you,' and they ask me 'What is his name?' what shall I say to them? God said to Moses, 'I AM WHO I AM.' And he said, 'Say this to the people of Israel, I AM has sent me to you.'"

Turning to John 8:56-58, we find a narrative of Jesus' encounter with certain Jews regarding His identity. Claiming the lineage of Abraham, they thought that name dropping would earn them a higher position of authority than Jesus held. He affirmed that they were indeed Abraham's children physically, but certainly not his spiritual descendants.

> "Your father Abraham rejoiced that he would see my day. He saw it and was glad." So the Jews said to him, "You are not yet fifty years old, and have you seen Abraham?" Jesus said to them "Truly, truly, I say to you, before Abraham was, I am." So they picked up stones to throw at him.

Jesus claimed to be the "I Am" of the Old Testament, the eternal, self-existent God. He also claimed that in some sense, Abraham anticipated His coming in the future. The Jewish opposition certainly believed that Jesus' claim was one of deity, for they tried to stone Him.

Jesus Claimed to Forgive Sins as God Forgives Sins

What's the big deal about Jesus claiming to forgive sins? When someone wrongs us as humans, we forgive, right? When Jesus healed the crippled man in Mark 2:5-7 and asserted that his sins were forgiven, are we to take it to mean that Jesus forgave his sins as all humans are supposed to do with others? (e.g., Matt. 6:14-15)

A closer look shows that there is something distinct about Jesus' claim. Imagine I walked up to you, having never met you before, and asserted, "Your sins are forgiven." You would laugh at me and say, "Who do you think you are?" Why? Because as a stranger, I have no right or authority to forgive all your sins. In fact, it would be silly to think someone would say such a thing to a complete stranger. This is exactly what Jesus claimed to do, though. He claimed to forgive the man's sins as God forgives sin, with the authority of deity.

Jesus Claimed to Be One with the Father

In John 10:30-33 Jesus said that He and the Father were one. Jehovah's Witnesses argue that Jesus merely claimed to be one in purpose with the Father. But this was not His claim, as can be quickly discerned just from the passage itself. Jesus claimed to be one *in nature* with the Father. How do we know? Once again, the Jews picked up stones to kill the blasphemer because He claimed to be equal with God.

Regarding this passage, they suggest that Jesus' claim to be one with God was an assertion that He was one in purpose with God. But this is clearly not the case. We know for certain that these Jews recognized that Jesus claimed to be God, because they tried to kill Him for this blasphemy. Jehovah's Witnesses have said to me, "But the Jewish leaders were wrong about Christ being God." That misses the point. The question is whether they understood His claim to be a claim to deity. Obviously, they did.

But if Jesus claimed to be God, why did He say, "The Father is greater than I" in John 14:28? As relates to his *deity*, Jesus is equal with the Father (John 10:30). But as relates to His *humanity* and function, the Father is greater. This is the same reason He said in Matthew 24:36 that the Son did not know the time of His return, only the Father knew. He did not choose to access knowledge in His humanity that He could have known in His deity.

Philippians 2:5-8 explains that Jesus had two natures: divine and human. When He emptied Himself, He did not empty Himself of His deity. Rather, He emptied Himself of the glory due Him and which had been His before the world began. He humbled Himself and added to His deity human flesh.

Jesus Accepted Worship

If Jesus was not God and accepted worship, He would have been a blasphemer. In Revelation 19:9-10, when John bowed to an angel, the angel immediately told him to get up, that he was a fellow servant and not to be worshipped. When Peter met Cornelius, the soldier bowed to worship Peter. Peter immediately refused, saying he was just a man (Acts 10:25-26). And yet Jesus never corrected anyone for worshipping Him (see Matt. 2:11, Matt. 14:33, Matt. 28:9, Matt. 20:20), showing that He did claim to be God in the flesh.

A poignant scene clearly reveals Jesus' acceptance, and even expectation, of worship. Disciple Thomas had been absent from the Lord's previous appearance and when his colleagues claimed they had seen the Lord alive, Thomas, not having witnessed the appearance, said he would not believe unless he actually saw the nail imprints, touched the nail imprints, and touched His speared side. A week later, the disciples met together again and Jesus appeared to them. This time

Thomas was present. Jesus offered the specific three evidences that Thomas had requested: "Put your finger here, and see my hands; and put out your hand, and place it in my side. Do not disbelieve, but believe." Thomas answered him, "My Lord and my God!" (John 20:27-28)

Skeptics have said that Thomas merely exclaimed in a similar way that we do, but not because he believed. They need to read the next verse, because Jesus said, "Have you believed because you have seen me? Blessed are those who have not seen and yet have believed" (v. 29). His proclamation confirmed his belief in Christ.

Given the fact that He claimed to be God, why was Jesus not more direct and overt in His assertion of His deity? The Jewish religious leaders set out to kill Christ once the crowds started following after Him, seeking miracles, and especially after He had raised Lazarus from the dead. Of course, they plotted to *re*-kill Lazarus, as well, which was an exercise in futility, given the fact that Jesus had already shown He could make dead people un-dead. At any rate, as the Lord Himself made clear, no one took His life from Him, He gave it willingly (John 7:1-8, 10:18). So, He would accomplish His mission and trek to the cross in His own timing, not according to the insidious timing of opponents. He also may have wished not to override human will. Those who would reject Him, could do so freely. He sought to persuade but not coerce them.

Jesus Claimed to Be the Son of Man

Matthew (26:63-66) records that during Jesus' interrogation before the chief priests prior to His crucifixion, high priest Caiaphas asked the Lord,

> "Are you the Christ, the Son of the Blessed?" And Jesus said, "I am, and you will see the Son of Man seated at the right hand of Power, and coming with the clouds of heaven." And the high priest tore his garments and said, "What further witnesses do we need? You have heard his blasphemy. What is your decision?" And they all condemned him as deserving death.

By referring to Himself as the Son of Man Jesus was not merely saying that He identified with humanity. He certainly did identify with us in becoming human to stand in our place and receive the holy wrath of God against our sin. But "Son of Man" was a phrase used by Daniel to refer to Messiah in Daniel 7:13-14:

With the clouds of heaven there came one like a son of man, and he came to the Ancient of Days and was presented before him. And to him was given dominion and glory and a kingdom, that all peoples, nations, and languages should serve him; his dominion is an everlasting dominion, which shall not pass away, and his kingdom one that shall not be destroyed.

This One would reign over an eternal kingdom as God. Everyone in the room knew exactly what Jesus was claiming here. That is why Caiaphas tore his garment, accused the Savior of blasphemy, and condemned Him to death.

Jesus' New Testament Writers Believed He Was God

Not only did Jesus claim to be God in the New Testament, but also His disciples, who wrote the New Testament, believed and claimed He was God. While the faith of the Lord's disciples was often flecked with immaturity, those closest to Him believed He was the very Son of God, the promised Messiah, and God in the flesh. Let's look at several examples.

While in Caesarea Philippi Jesus asked His disciples who people said that He was. Several possible identities were suggested. He then pointedly asked them, "But who do you say that I am?" **Peter** responded, "You are the Christ, the Son of the living God" (Matt. 16:16). Peter proclaimed that Jesus was Messiah, the promised one of God. As we will show in the discussion of Christ's fulfillment of prophecies, Messiah was presented in the Old Testament as both fully human and fully God. John the Beloved, also in the inner circle of three that included brothers James and John (sons of Zebedee), and Peter, asserted that Christ was "the Word" and that the "Word was God" (John 1:1).

While Jehovah's Witnesses insist that the passage could be rendered, "The Word was a God," the best interpretation, according to New Testament scholar David Alan Black is, "It was God that the Word was," making clear John's assertion that Christ was indeed God.[175] In John 1:14 the apostle asserts that Jesus was also the "Son from the Father," who became flesh and lived among humans. Then, in verse 29 the apostle John describes John the Baptist's witness confirming the identity of Jesus Christ as the promised Messiah. On seeing Jesus, John the Baptist proclaimed, "Behold, the Lamb of God, who takes away the sin of the world!"

James, the half-brother of Christ, did not believe in Jesus as Messiah-God during the Lord's life and ministry (John 7:5). But after the resurrection, Paul reports that the Lord appeared to James (1 Cor. 15:3-8). James was transformed and became one of the primary witnesses in Jerusalem (Acts 15:13-21). He writes in James 1:1 that he is a servant of the "Lord Jesus Christ," and then in 5:8, he urges his readers to be patient and to prepare their hearts for "the coming of the Lord," saying also, "the Judge is standing at the door." James clearly affirms Jesus Christ as His master, as Lord, and as returning Judge.

The **writer of Hebrews** says regarding Jesus, "In these last days he has spoken to us by his Son" (1:2). He goes on to describe Jesus, saying, "He is the radiance of the glory of God and the exact imprint of his nature, and he upholds the universe by the word of his power. After making purification for sins, he sat down at the right hand of the Majesty on high, having become as much superior to angels as the name he has inherited is more excellent than theirs" (1:2-4). Hebrews 2:7 explains that when Jesus became human, He was temporarily "a little lower than the angels." At the same time, says the Hebrews writer, He has the nature of God, sustains the entire universe by His will, and through obedience to the cross' demands, He has been exalted to His rightful position of authority.

He then says, "For to which of the angels did God ever say, 'You are my Son, today I have begotten you?' Or again, 'I will be to him a father, and he shall be to me a son?'" (1:5). While some argue that this means that the Father created the Son, this phrase actually refers to the Son's privileged relationship with the Father. As Daniel Mann, of the Christian Research Institute points out, since the Father was already speaking to the Son when He made the comment, the Son was already in existence when the Father said, "Today I have begotten you."[176]

The better interpretation of this statement is that "begotten" refers to enthronement. Several insights point us this direction. The statement is actually a quote of Psalm 2:6-7, which is a messianic psalm of David. Speaking of the "LORD's anointed," which in the immediate sense was David, and in the remote sense, the Messiah, David records a conversation between himself and God: "'I have set my King in Zion, my holy hill.' I will tell of the decree: The LORD said to me, 'You are my Son; today I have begotten you.'" Notice in this psalm, as well as in Hebrews, the individual to whom God says, "Today I have begotten you," is a person who already exists. David sees the LORD as speaking this to him, and the New Testament verifies that Jesus the Son is the ultimate fulfillment of this affirmation. Therefore, God Himself has exalted His Chosen Servant and in this sense, has "begotten," not "birthed" Him.[177]

Finally, the Hebrews writer clearly distinguishes between the angels and Jesus, saying, "But of the Son he says, 'Your throne, O God, is forever and ever'" (1:7). The passage could be no clearer: The Son Himself is called God. Further, His rule and authority is eternal.

The apostle **Paul** says of Jesus in Colossians 1:15-18, "He is the image of the invisible God, the firstborn of all creation. For by him all things were created, in heaven and on earth, visible and invisible, whether thrones or dominions or rulers or authorities—all things were created through him and for him. And he is before all things, and in him all things hold together."

The concepts of "image" and of "firstborn" need to be fleshed out in order to affirm Paul's intended meaning that Christ was God in the flesh. The Greek word for "image" (*eikōn*) was used to convey two nuanced meanings. The first idea was that the image "represented and symbolized what the object pictured."[178] The word was often used in this way when referring to images imprinted on coins. If this had been Paul's intention, he would have said that "Jesus was the symbol of deity." In the second way the word was used, however, the image "brought with it the actual presence of the object." This is Paul's intention here. "The point is that in Christ the invisible God became visible." While Adam was *created* in the image of God, "Jesus was unique in that he *manifested* the image of God" [italics mine].[179]

The concept of "firstborn" has also been misunderstood and misrepresented by sects such as Jehovah's Witnesses to say that Jesus was a created being. The argument is not new. In the fourth century, a heretic named Arius proposed that Jesus was the firstborn, meaning the first created, of all created things. Thus, Jesus was a created being, but the preeminent created being who created everything else. His views were condemned as heretical.[180]

The term "firstborn" can refer to the first child born to parents. But in Scripture, the term is also used for kings, on whom God bestowed the preeminent status of "firstborn," which indicated their favored position before God. In Psalm 89:27, speaking of David, God says, "I will make him the firstborn, the highest of the kings of the earth," illustrating that the term "firstborn" often referred, not to a child's order of birth, but rather the privileged status God *bestowed* on His favored one. Jesus is the preeminent One, over all creation, including all of the angels.

Finally, **Luke** said of Jesus Christ's birth, "For unto you is born this day in the city of David a Savior, who is Christ the Lord" (Luke 2:11). When healing the Gadarene demoniac, Luke's account in chapter eight asserts that the demons called out to Jesus, "What have you to do with me, Jesus, son of the Most high God?" (v. 28) Luke's story line throughout his Gospel and also Acts affirms Jesus Christ's authority over nature, demons, sickness, and death. He also asserts that Jesus stated that the entire Old Testament was written about Him, in Luke 24:44.

We have seen that Jesus Christ Himself claimed many times to be God. Further, Christ's followers clearly affirmed that Jesus Christ was God in the flesh, Redeemer of mankind, and King of the universe. Given the strong evidence supporting these claims, we will now turn to the evidence that Jesus proved Himself to be all that He claimed to be.

20

Did Jesus Confirm His Deity by Fulfilling Old Testament Prophecies?

If sincerity would get you to heaven, then the terrorists of 9-11 would be a shoe-in. No one doubted that they sincerely believed that what they called martyrdom would earn them peace with Allah and great personal pleasure and joy in the life to come. So, by the same token, the fact that Jesus believed Himself to be God, and the New Testament writers sincerely believed that He was God, does not prove that He was God. While it is important to show that this is what they sincerely believed in order to demonstrate they were not charlatans or characters of disrepute, we need to show more. We have to present evidence that demonstrates that His own claims and His disciples' assertions about His deity were true.

One of the greatest dangers of solely focusing on what the New Testament says about Jesus is that we begin to see Him as arriving on history's scene in the first century A.D. But it is the historic Christian belief that Jesus pre-existed the creation of the universe as eternal God. His advent was orchestrated before the foundation of the world, and ancient history is filled with promises that He, this Messiah, would come and free people from their sins.

Beginning with Moses' writing of the Law, all the way to the last book of Malachi, Jesus Christ was revealed in at least 60 major Old Testament prophecies written hundreds of years before He was born. A look at even a handful of these prophecies progressively narrows the field of candidates for the Jewish Messiah to the point that the person spoken about could be none other than Jesus Christ of Nazareth who lived in the first century A.D.

Think of an upside-down triangle with the point directed downward. As we start in Genesis looking at prophecies, we will begin at the broad top of the triangle, signifying that the prophecies are general in nature. As we continue through the prophetic writings of the Old Testament, we see that they become progressively more specific, until we reach the bottom of the triangle where the lines converge in a point, zeroing in on a single person in history who qualifies as the promised Messiah-God. Let's look at a few.

Fully Human and Defeater of Satan

Genesis 3:15, the passage often called the *proto-evangelion* or first gospel message, says that God cursed the serpent and said, "I will put enmity between and the woman and between your offspring and her offspring; he shall bruise you head, and you shall bruise his heel." The "offspring" or "Seed" (NKJV), which many scholars believe refers to Messiah, would demonstrate victory over Satan and his efforts to thwart God's salvation plan.

Significant also is that the Seed would be born of woman. Normally, men supply the seed. But, in Messiah's case, God provided the life-seed. Messiah would be born of woman and was fully human.

From the Semitic Ethnic Group

In Genesis 12:3 the scope of possible identities for this one who would defeat Satan narrows to the ethnic group of people who became the Jewish nation when the LORD spoke to Abraham and promised: "And you shall be a blessing. . . . And in you all the families of the earth shall be blessed." Indeed, not only did the Jewish people received the gospel, but also the Gentiles would be grafted in as recipients of the wondrous message of salvation. Thus, Abraham became a blessing to all people groups as the progenitor of Messiah.

From the Tribe of Judah

Genesis 49:8-10 explains that Messiah wouldn't come from the descendants of just any of Jacob's 12 sons, but specifically from the tribe of Judah:

Judah, you are he whom your brothers shall praise; Your hand shall be on the neck of your enemies; Your father's children shall bow down before you. Judah is a lion's whelp; From the prey, my son, you have gone up. He bows down, he lies down as a lion; And as a lion, who shall rouse him? The scepter shall not depart from Judah, Nor a lawgiver from between his feet, Until Shiloh comes.

In Revelation 5:5 it is the "Lion of the tribe of Judah, the Root of David" who "prevailed to open the scroll and to loose its seven seals." Thus, the kingly line as represented by the royal scepter would remain in the house, and ultimately the nation, of Judah. But there would come a time when the authority would be transferred to Shiloh, the word either being a title or a name for Messiah. Wayne Jackson of the publication, *The Christian Courier*, asserts that the people of Judah maintained a national identity even when subjugated by other nations, during which various governors, administrators and priest-kings functioned in leadership roles until Herod Archaelaus was removed from power during the time of Christ.[181]

From the House of David

In 2 Samuel 7:12-16, we see what many evangelical scholars call a dual fulfillment prophecy, one immediate and one remote. God says to David,

When your days are fulfilled and you lie down with your fathers, I will raise up your offspring after you, who shall come from your body, and I will establish his kingdom. He shall build a house for my name, and I will establish the throne of his kingdom forever.

Now, this passage, which extends through verse 16, includes a reference to Solomon, which explains why the following verses 14-15 say, "I will be to him a father, and he shall be to me a son. When he commits iniquity, I will discipline him . . . but my steadfast love will not depart from him, as I took it from Saul."

While Solomon would sin, the remote fulfillment by Messiah focuses on the "forever" of Solomon's kingdom as fulfilled in Messiah Jesus. The New Testament writers Matthew and Luke confirm this in their genealogies. In Matthew 1, Jesus' lineage is traced through David via his legal adoptive father, Joseph. Then, Luke 3 traces his blood relation to David through his biological mother, Mary, confirming the remote fulfillment of the prophecy.

Born of a Virgin

Another dual fulfillment passage, Isaiah 7:14, speaks of a virgin who will bear a son who is called Immanuel, which means "God with us." "Therefore the Lord himself will give you a sign. Behold, the virgin shall conceive and bear a son, and shall call his name Immanuel." Skeptics make much of the word *almah* simply referring to a young woman who was a virgin at the time she became pregnant, not to a woman who remained a virgin, even in her conception.

While there was evidently an immediate fulfillment through a young woman who bore a son during the time of Ahaz, New Testament writer Matthew (1:23) verifies that Mary's pregnancy fulfilled this prophecy. Mary's conception occurred via the Holy Spirit, says Matthew, and Mary was indeed a virgin at conception and during her pregnancy. Joseph and Mary did not have intimate relations until after Jesus was born (Matt. 1:25).

Born in Bethlehem of Judah

In Micah 5:2 the prophet foretold, "But you, O Bethlehem Ephrathah, who are too little to be among the clans of Judah, from you shall come forth for me one who is to be ruler in Israel, whose coming forth is from of old, from ancient days." Micah served God as prophet about 730 B.C. and his ministry overlapped with his contemporaries, Isaiah, who preached in Judah, and Hosea, who prophesied in Israel. His messages addressed both Judah and Israel, with a focus on Judah.[182]

Micah's prediction that Messiah would be born in Bethlehem of Judah rules out another Bethlehem near Nazareth as the location for Messiah's birth. Bethlehem is located about five miles south of Jerusalem. Ephrathah was the town's ancient name, or for the area in which it was located. Jacob's wife Rachel died in childbirth on the road to Bethlehem (Gen. 35:16-19). During the time of the judges, Ruth the Moabitess followed her mother-in-law, Naomi, to Bethlehem (Ruth 1:19), and there married Boaz, becoming King David's great-grandmother. During David's time the Philistines used the site as a garrison for their soldiers (2 Sam. 23:14), and David called it by its ancient name Ephrathah in Psalm 132:6. The town fell into obscurity until Micah mentioned its surprising destiny as the birthplace of Messiah (5:2).[183]

In the New Testament, Matthew (2:6) asserted that Micah's prophecy about Bethlehem was fulfilled in the circumstances of Jesus Christ's birth. When Mary and Joseph traveled to Bethlehem for the census (enrollment) late in Mary's pregnancy, Jesus was delivered while they were there (Matt. 2:1-2). Micah's prophecy is so specific as to weed out the majority of potential candidates who could possibly be Messiah. And there's more.

Execution by Piercing

In Zechariah 12:10 the prophet reveals an event that will occur at the end time when Messiah returns:

And I will pour out on the house of David and the inhabitants of Jerusalem a spirit of grace and pleas for mercy, so that, when they look on me, on him whom they have pierced, they shall mourn for him, as one mourns for an only child, and weep bitterly over him, as one weeps over a firstborn.

Zechariah was likely from a priestly family who returned to Jerusalem about 520 B.C. with the first group of exile returnees from the Babylonian exile, under the leadership of Zerubbabel. One of his roles was to encourage the people to complete the building of the temple, a project that had been delayed about 16 years.[184]

In one of his prophecies Zechariah said that there would come a day when God's people would return to Him and to the one whom He sent, Messiah. They would grieve over the one whom they pierced. Piercing and nailing were not forms of Jewish execution, as we have noted, and yet Zechariah, as well as the psalmist in Psalm 22:16-18, both mention a form of execution in which piercing was involved. The psalmist said, "For dogs encompass me; a company of evildoers encircles me; they have pierced my hands and feet—I can count all my bones—they stare and gloat over me; they divide my garments among them, and for my clothing they cast lots." Hundreds of years after these prophecies, Christ was crucified. Luke 23:33, 24:39, and John 20:25, say Christ's hands and feet were fastened to the cross by nailing. John 20:25-28 also affirms Thomas' demand to see the wounds of the piercing in order to believe.

One of the most poignant narratives in the Bible is also one of the most simple and direct. John stands at the foot of the Savior's cross. The Lord has given him responsibility to take care of his mom, Mary. The Lord then dies, and John makes a simple observation that he has no idea would be scrutinized meticulously in coming centuries: "But when they came to Jesus and saw that he was already dead, they did not break his legs. But one of the soldiers pierced his side with a spear, and at once there came out blood and water" (John 19:33-34). The fact that blood, then water, flowed from the Savior's side signified death from one of several proposed catastrophic physiological events, such as piercing of the pericardial sac, which filled with watery fluid. Regardless of the exact mechanism of death, the clot had already separated from the serum, the clear part of the blood, which John described as water.

John watched as his friend and Master was pierced for our transgressions and simply recorded what he saw. And what he saw confirmed that Messiah would die by a means of execution alien to Jewish culture at the time the prophecies were written. But the prophets didn't write their own insights. They wrote what was revealed to them, even when it didn't fit their expectations.

Fully God

Isaiah 9:6 tells us that Messiah would not only be human, but would also be fully God: "For to us a child is born, to us a son is given; and the government shall be upon his shoulder, and his name shall be called Wonderful Counselor, Mighty God, Everlasting Father, Prince of Peace." The Son from eternity existed, so as Son, He is not born. He *is* born, however, as a human child. His names speak to His eternal wisdom, deity, authority over all eternity, and His role in restoring peace between God and man. The term "Everlasting Father" does not refer to Messiah being the same person as Father God, which would be a confusion of the persons of the Triune Godhead. Each person is God substance, nature, or "stuffness." The God substance exists in three personal relations as Father, Son, and Spirit. So the term "Everlasting Father" or "Father of Eternity" refers to Messiah's ultimate authority and dominion over all of time and eternity.

Jehovah's Witnesses insist that Jehovah alone is "Almighty God" and that the reference to Messiah being "Mighty God" means that Jesus as Messiah was not fully God: "The Hebrew Scriptures are consistently clear in showing that there is but one Almighty God, the Creator of all things and the Most High, whose name is Jehovah."[185] But in Jeremiah 32:16-18 Jeremiah said, "I prayed to the LORD saying, . . . 'You show steadfast love to thousands, but you repay the guilt of fathers to their children after them, O great and mighty God, whose name is the LORD of hosts,'" clearly referring to God Jehovah or Yahweh. In other words, Jeremiah speaks to the LORD—Yahweh—and calls Him "Mighty God."

Does the Bible Contain a Prophecy About Muhammad?

Muslims often claim that the Bible prophesied the coming of Muhammad. The main scripture they cite is Deuteronomy 18:15: "The LORD your God will raise up for you a prophet like me from among you, from your brothers—it is to him you shall listen." The argument from Muslim apologists is that since Ishmael was the brother of Isaac, the prophet would be raised up from the Ishmaelites, or from the Arab nation. Setting aside the counter argument that not all Arabs are descended from Ishmael, it only requires a cursory look at the context of the passage to see that Moses was not referring to someone outside of the people of Israel.

In 18:1-2, immediately preceding the verse in question, God says that the Levitical priests will not receive land inheritance but rather shall be provided food through the sacrifices of the people. "They shall have no inheritance among their brothers; the LORD is their inheritance, as he promised them." Clearly, the brothers to whom he is referring are Israelites, not Ishmaelites, or anyone else outside the twelve tribes of Israel. In the first New Testament martyr's speech given by the disciple Stephen and recorded by Luke in Acts 3, Stephen verified it was Jesus Christ about whom Moses spoke when the promise was made in Deuteronomy.

Non-messianic Jews, who don't believe that Jesus is Messiah, take a different view of the Old Testament prophecies. I visited with a friend of my husband's, who is a Reformed Jew and able to read Hebrew.

I asked him to read aloud to me Psalm 22 in Hebrew. We have already mentioned that this passage discusses the form of execution of someone by piercing. But who is the someone? When the gentlemen finished reading the psalm aloud to me, I asked him to whom the passage was referring. Like many Jews he said, "The nation of Israel."

I agree with him that many Old Testament prophecies can be viewed as referring to the nation of Israel. But not all of them. Some of them such as Psalm 22 have an individual in view. An important example of the prophecy pointing toward an individual rather than a nation is Isaiah 53:1-12. Read the passage and see if you can identify descriptive sections that could not be referring to the nation of Israel, but rather seem to point to an individual person:

Who has believed what he has heard from us?
And to whom has the arm of the Lord been revealed?

For he grew up before him like a young plant,
and like a root out of dry ground;
he had no form or majesty that we should look at him,
and no beauty that we should desire him.

He was despised and rejected by men,
a man of sorrows and acquainted with grief;
and as one from whom men hide their faces
he was despised, and we esteemed him not.

Surely he has borne our griefs
and carried our sorrows;
yet we esteemed him stricken,
smitten by God, and afflicted.

But he was pierced for our transgressions;
he was crushed for our iniquities;
upon him was the chastisement that brought us peace,
and with his wounds we are healed.

All we like sheep have gone astray;
we have turned—every one—to his own way;
and the Lord has laid on him
the iniquity of us all.

He was oppressed, and he was afflicted,
yet he opened not his mouth;
like a lamb that is led to the slaughter,
and like a sheep that before its shearers is silent,
so he opened not his mouth.

By oppression and judgment he was taken away;
and as for his generation, who considered
that he was cut off out of the land of the living,
stricken for the transgression of my people?

And they made his grave with the wicked
and with a rich man in his death,
although he had done no violence,
and there was no deceit in his mouth.

Yet it was the will of the Lord to crush him;
he has put him to grief;
when his soul makes an offering for guilt,
he shall see his offspring; he shall prolong his days;
the will of the Lord shall prosper in his hand.

Out of the anguish of his soul he shall see and be satisfied;
by his knowledge shall the righteous one, my servant,
make many to be accounted righteous,
and he shall bear their iniquities.

Therefore I will divide him a portion with the many,
and he shall divide the spoil with the strong,
because he poured out his soul to death
and was numbered with the transgressors;
yet he bore the sin of many,
and makes intercession for the transgressors.

It is true that the nation of Israel has been despised and rejected. But this passage cannot refer to the nation of Israel for several reasons. Israel has never borne the griefs on behalf of another. Messiah bore our griefs and carried our sorrows, serving as our intercessor. Israel has never been pierced for another's transgressions, has never received punishment that brought others' peace, and has never healed others' wounds through vicarious suffering. Moreover, when persecuted, Israel has never been silent like a sheep before its shearers.

This passage clearly reveals Messiah, an individual who would serve as intercessor for His people. Interestingly, before Jesus' incarnation, even Jewish rabbis believed that this prophetic passage referred to an individual. The Gospel writers each described Christ's crucifixion. Reading through the Gospel accounts of Jesus' suffering, death, and resurrection reveals specific fulfillment of the descriptions of Messiah in Isaiah 53:1-12 (see Matt. 26-27, Mark 15-16; John 18-19, Luke 22-23).

21

Did Jesus' Life Bear Marks of Perfection and Miracles?

We have already shown the evidence that the New Testament is historically reliable. So, we can legitimately use scriptures as evidence supporting the claim that Jesus claimed to be God and that His life bore the marks of the miraculous and of perfection of character.

Jesus' Perfect Character

John the apostle said that the Word became flesh, lived among men, and that the eyewitnesses observed His visible glory. That glory, he said, reflected the glory of the Father. He affirmed that the Word was filled with both grace (of the New Covenant superseding the Law) and truth (recall that Isaiah said there was no deceit at all in Messiah).

He was perfect in character and able to restore the holiness that humanity had lost in sin, giving us a glimpse of the Father. Three lines of evidence within the trustworthy New Testament documents reveal that Christ was sinless. His closest friends believed He was sinless, He claimed in His own words and actions to be without sin, and even His enemies were unable to convict Him of any wrongdoing, which some of His enemies even acknowledged.

Jesus' Closest Friends Claimed He Was Sinless

It is axiomatic that the closer you get to another human the more you see his or her faults, failures, and frailty. Yet, the closer Christ's disciples got to Him, the longer they walked with Him, the more they watched Him suffering, hated, maligned, mistreated, and mocked, the more convinced they became of His perfection.

The apostle Peter said of his Lord, "He committed no sin, neither was deceit found in his mouth," (1 Peter 2:22), applying the messianic phrase of Isaiah 53 to Jesus. I know several very godly people, but about not a one could I ever make such a statement.

The apostle Paul said of Him, "For our sake he made him to be sin who knew no sin, so that in him we might become the righteousness of God" (2 Cor. 5:21). Not only is our Savior without sin Himself, but also He took on the mantle of sin in our place. Sin was alien to His personality, yet He willingly suffered the full and justified wrath of holy God against our sin. How great a love is this!

The writer of Hebrews said, "For we do not have a high priest who is unable to sympathize with our weaknesses, but one who in every respect has been tempted as we are, yet without sin" (4:15). We should not think that Jesus' sinlessness was easily accomplished because He was God. He was also human, and thus, His perfection was tried and proved in His humanity. This passage also teaches us that He understands. He truly understands our predicament, and "He remembers that we are dust" (Psalm 103:14), because He has walked our journey.

The apostle John was Jesus' closest friend. Called the "beloved disciple," the Lord loved and trusted him so much that as He was dying, He gave John the responsibility of taking care of His precious mother (John 19:27). John said about Jesus (1:1-5),

In the beginning was the Word, and the Word was with God, and the Word was God. He was in the beginning with God. All things were made through him, and without him was not any thing made that was made. In him was life, and the life was the light of men. The light shines in the darkness, and the darkness has not overcome it.

He tells the reader the specific identity of the Word in verse 14: "And the Word became flesh and dwelt among us, and we have seen his glory, glory as of the only Son from the Father, full of grace and truth."

In John's view, Jesus Christ, the Word who was with God and was God from eternity, was also the Creator and the light that no darkness could overpower. What higher praise and honor could be attributed to any person?

Jesus Claimed to Be Sinless

In confrontation with the Jews one day, Jesus said, "Which one of you convicts me of sin? If I tell the truth, why do you not believe me? Whoever is of God hears the words of God. The reason why you do not hear them is that you are not of God" (John 8:46-47). Not only did He claim to be sinless in this passage, but He also claimed to be from God and said He spoke truth.

In Mark 10:17-22 a young man approached Jesus to ask Him a pressing question: "Good Teacher, what must I do to inherit eternal life?" And Jesus said to him, "Why do you call me good? No one is good except God alone" (vv. 17-18). Some have questioned why Jesus would deny His deity in this statement, saying that only God was good so the young man shouldn't call Him good. This is actually not what the statement means. In fact, Jesus was saying, *Look, no person is good. Only God is truly good. So, when you call me good, you are calling me God.* From the authoritative position of God, He then told the man what he didn't want to hear. His possessions were his god. When confronted with his sin by God in the flesh, the young man walked away sad, because he was not willing to submit.

Jesus' Enemies Found No Sin in Him

John 19:4-7 says that after flogging Jesus and placing a crown of thorns on His head, Pilate presented Him to the crowd and said,

"See, I am bringing him out to you that you may know that I find no guilt in him." So Jesus came out, wearing the crown of thorns and the purple robe. Pilate said to them, "Behold the man!" When the chief priests and the officers saw him, they cried out, "Crucify him, crucify him!" Pilate said to them, "Take him yourselves and crucify him, for I find no guilt in him." The Jews answered him, "We have a law, and according to that law he ought to die because he has made himself the Son of God."

Pilate could find no wrongdoing in the Lord. The Jews who accused Him of wrongdoing did not claim He had committed any wrong against any man. In fact, they recognized that He did miracles, but were angered that He drew the respect and awe of the crowds they coveted in order to maintain control. So, they accused Him, not of any wrongdoing for which He could legally be prosecuted, but for blasphemy, because He called Himself the Son of God. Of course, Jesus did not commit blasphemy if He was who He claimed to be.

Jesus' Life Was Marked by Miracles

We have already established that if the theistic God exists, miracles must be possible. We have also examined evidence that the New Testament writers, who were not given to imaginative fairy tales, and who were of honorable character, recorded the narratives describing what Jesus said and did. The Gospels record approximately 35 miracles performed by the Lord. He demonstrated power and authority over nature, over demons, over sickness, and over death. Never has another human being's life been so marked by the miraculous.

Jesus Himself explained more than once the purpose of His miracles. On one occasion, John the Baptist, the messenger who prepared the way before the Anointed One, sat in prison. It was John's darkest hour. Matthew 11:4-6 records that he sent word to the Lord asking if He was the One or if they should expect another Messiah. Jesus said,

> Go and tell John what you hear and see: the blind receive their sight and the lame walk, lepers are cleansed and the deaf hear, and the dead are raised up, and the poor have good news preached to them. And blessed is the one who is not offended by me.

Jesus didn't say, "Just have faith." He presented the evidence supporting His claim to Messiahship, evidence that He Himself was the God-Man who came to save people from their sins.

In John 10:22-39 John the apostle records that at the Feast of Dedication, when Jesus walked in the temple, the Jews gathered around Him, baiting Him with the challenge, "How long will you keep us in suspense? If you are the Christ, tell us plainly" (v. 24). Jesus responded that He had told them exactly who He was but they did not believe Him.

He then asserted, "I and the Father are one" (v. 30), after which the Jews picked up stones to stone Him for blasphemy.

He then issued them a challenge (vv. 37-39):

> "If I am not doing the works of my Father, then do not believe me; but if I do them, even though you do not believe me, believe the works, that you may know and understand that the Father is in me and I am in the Father." Again they sought to arrest Him, but He escaped from their hands.

The works—the miracles—said Jesus, were performed to open the understanding of those who could appraise them and recognize that He was from God. But it was their choice, as it is ours, to accept or reject the evidence.

Power Over Nature

Near Capernaum, Jesus had spent the day teaching by Lake Galilee from a boat, because He was pressed upon by the crowd, many of whom He healed. It was early evening. He was exhausted. He instructed His disciples to push off the boat, saying, "Let us go over to the other side" (Mark 4:35). They pushed off. On the other side, Jesus would heal men from demonic possession, but of course, the disciples didn't know that yet. And they had a storm to endure before they saw Him heal.

My own boat ride on the Sea of Galilee on our Israel trip was exquisitely beautiful. The day was warm and sunny, with a gossamer haze hovering over the coastline. The lake is about 12 miles long and 7 miles wide, sunken in a deep rift 680 feet below sea level between hilly ranges that rise to an elevation of 2000 feet.[186] When the cool, dry air of the hills hits the warm, moist air rising from the lake, a blustery storm can develop quickly, and this is exactly what happened in Mark's account (Mark 5: 35-41, Matt. 8:23-27, Luke 8:22-25).[187]

The disciples became fearful and Jesus was worn out, asleep in the stern. They awakened Him with an accusation, "Don't you care?" When Jesus said, "Peace, be still," the Greek suggests He said something like, "Hush now. Be still." The waves settled and quiet descended. The disciples were stunned, as we would be, that even the weather submitted to Christ's command. The significance of Christ's authority over the weather was not lost on them. They likely knew that in Psalm 107:29 it was Yahweh who stilled the storm. So, they wondered aloud, "Who is this that even the winds and the waves obey him?" (Mark 4:41) The answer is, He is God in the flesh, Creator of the universe, through whose word the waters and the winds came to be.

Power Over Demons

Once Jesus and His disciples had reached the other side of the lake, they were met by a naked man (actually two according to Matthew, but we hear the words of only one), who lived among the graves in the region of the Gadarenes. The incident is shared by all of the Synoptic Gospel writers: Matthew 8:28-34, Mark 8:23-27, and Luke 8:26-29 (synoptic meaning "same eye" for the commonalities among Matthew, Mark, and Luke).

Demons were created as angels, but chose to follow Satan in his rebellion against God. While many today argue that people with epilepsy or other ailments were mistakenly thought to be demon possessed, Luke 9:1 makes a distinction between the disciples being able to heal sicknesses by the authority of Christ and being able to cast out demons by Christ's authority. It is true that physical symptoms accompanied demon possession, as the demons sought to destroy the person, body and soul. But demons actually spoke, identified themselves, recognized Jesus as the Son of God, and made requests, showing personhood. In this incident they requested to be cast into a herd of pigs, and Christ granted the request, sending the pigs into a headlong dash over a cliff into the water below.

Why would demons be more active in the time of Christ? Because Jesus' entrance into the earthly realm with His presence, His humanity, His miracles, His sacrificial death, and His resurrection, manifested God's kingdom breaking into our world, the very action the demonic cohort opposed. Regardless, the Lord held power and authority over them, and Luke 9:1 also explains that Jesus delegated authority over demons to His disciples.

The transformation of the demon-possessed man was immediate and stark. He went from a blithering, incoherent, violent, naked outcast, to sitting calmly and speaking with clarity. Such is the transformational work of Christ in our lives.

Some will raise as a possible contradiction that Matthew mentions two demon-possessed men, while Luke and Mark mention only one. A contradiction would only occur if Mark and Luke insisted there was *only* one man, since if there were two, there had to be at least one, and that one was the more central character of the event.[188]

Power Over Sickness

Jesus was actually on His way to heal a young girl, the daughter of Jairus, when someone in the throng reached out and touched His garment (Luke 8:40-56). The brave woman had an uncontrollable bleeding problem, and no physician had been able to help her. Her life must have been one of unrelenting misery. But she believed. She believed that if she could only touch Jesus' garment she would be healed. When the Lord sensed the power had flowed from Him, He asked who had touched Him. Terrified, the woman confessed that she was the one who had touched His robe, and the bleeding had immediately stopped. The Lord praised her faith.

When the curse of sin fell like a dark smog over all of creation, one of the effects was broken bodies that just don't work right, bodies that start deteriorating from the moment we are born. Birth defects, genetic errors, organ failure, and cancerous growths plague the human race. Jesus Christ added to His deity humanity to identify with us and to take on the plague of sin and destroy it. His miracles of healing demonstrated God's compassion for the plight of humans and the Lord's identification with us. Moreover, His healing miracles drew a picture of what life was intended to be before the Fall. Health was ours. One day it will be again, and Jesus reminds us that He alone is the Great Physician.

Power Over Death

Jesus' most stunning miracle occurred four days after one of His dearest friends died. In John 11, the apostle records that the Lord had heard while He was in another town that Lazarus was sick. By the time He arrived on the scene, having intentionally waited so the greater glory of God could be revealed, not only had Lazarus died, but also he had been in the grave several days. When Jesus instructed bystanders to roll the stone away from the grave opening, Lazarus' sisters naturally voiced fear that the body's deterioration would produce a foul odor if the tombstone were removed.

John records that Jesus wept as He stood in front of His friend's tomb. Then He called Lazarus to come out of the grave. Out walked the dead-now-alive man, still garbed head to toe in the wrappings of death. Jesus did not perform the miracle to impress people. John explains and Jesus in His own words affirms that He did the miracle so that the people would believe (v. 42). This is the Savior who consistently provided evidence of His deity so that people would believe in Him.

There has never been another human like Jesus Christ. His life was marked by miracles demonstrating His power over nature, demons, sickness, and death. The miracles bore the attributes of true biblical miracles. They were instantaneous, reflected the power of God, and brought glory to Him. They reminded us that "God with Us" transforms lives and cares about our pain.

22

Did Jesus Physically Rise from the Dead?

The bodily resurrection of Jesus Christ from the dead is the distinguishing essential belief of Christianity. Everything else we hold to be true hinges upon this reality, and it is this belief that separates Christianity from all other religions in the world. Christ's resurrection is the very heart of the gospel (1 Cor. 15:1-4). If Christ did not rise, there is no "Good News," and as Paul, said, in 1 Corinthians 15:14-19, we should be pitied:

> If Christ has not been raised, then our preaching is in vain and your faith is in vain. We are even found to be misrepresenting God, because we testified about God that He raised Christ, whom He did not raise. . . . Your faith is futile and you are still in your sins. . . . If in Christ we have hope in this life only, we are of all people most to be pitied.

Belief in the resurrection is required for salvation, according to Romans 10:9-10. Jesus' resurrection of the body guarantees the resurrection of our bodies, as well (Phil. 3:20-21).

When we say that Jesus Christ rose from the dead, let's make sure we know what we are claiming. We are claiming that the same body that was beaten to a pulp, nailed to the cross, speared in the side, that bled blood and water—that same body that was pulled down limp from the cross, that Joseph of Arimathea placed in his family tomb, that was wrapped in linen cloths—that dead corpse without brain waves, breath, or heartbeat—after three days of rotting—suddenly inhaling a breath, and with a beating heart, stood up and walked out of the grave, alive forevermore.

The implication of the resurrection dwarfs any other hope held out by other belief systems. If true, then believers in Jesus Christ possess the same hope. For if Jesus, through His Father's will, accomplished His own resurrection from the dead, accomplishing ours is no feat at all. This is exactly what He promises. First Thessalonians 4:13-18 says that the dead in Christ shall rise first, that corpses now in the ground will reunite with their spirits in the fullness of glorified humanity, healed of the curse of sin and the scourge of sickness, brokenness, and death.

Our friend Judy has reached the final stages of her 12-year battle with cancer. Judy and Bob were told last week by her doctors that there is no more chemo, no more radiation, no more anything that can slow the process now. Randy and I met Judy and Bob in Seoul, Korea in 1980, where they served as missionaries and we came to volunteer for a couple of weeks. We have kept in touch and remained friends for the past 30 years.

This morning we received an email from them describing how they have chosen to spend their days until the Lord calls Judy home. Hospice has been called in to assist, but that is not the focus of their days. They awaken each morning to sit together on the back porch, listen to the birds, spend time with each other and the Lord, and meditate upon His sovereignty and the anticipation of heaven. Do they grieve? No doubt they weep, they cling to one another, and they pray. But they grieve with the sure hope that what Jesus did in His resurrection is also their destiny, heritage, and hope. The resurrection is the reason that we can confidently assert that although Judy will not survive, she *will* win her battle.

When we share with others that we believe in the resurrection of Jesus Christ, we are not sharing about an esoteric fact of history. When the dark days of life press in, and it is guaranteed that they will, Christ's resurrection is our reason for putting one foot in front of the other. We offer Christ to others so that they may know this real hope, as well.

He Really Rose

Jesus predicted at least three times that He would die and also that He would rise again (Matt. 16:21-23 [Mark 8:31-33, Luke 9:22]; Matt. 17:22-23 [Mark 9:30-32, Luke 9:43-45]; Matt. 20:17-19 [Mark 10:32-34, Luke 18:31-34]). Real resurrection presupposes real death. But some have argued that Jesus did not really die; He only fainted, or an imposter died in His place. Others have affirmed that He died but that He didn't really rise from the dead, offering a variety of innovative speculations about what could have actually happened. We need to remember that offering a *possible* explanation is not the same as offering a *reasonable* explanation supported by evidence. So, when people say, "Well, maybe it happened that . . ." or "It could have . . ." we can respond, with, "Many things are possible but not reasonable to believe. Let's look at the evidence to decide what is reasonable."

Jesus Died

Did He really die, or as some have suggested, did He just faint? John 19:34, as we have already seen, described that when the soldier pierced His side that blood, then water, poured out. Jesus was already dead, the clot having already formed, and the clear part of the blood, the serum, separating and flowing out behind the clot. It is rather like when you have your blood drawn and the red solid matter of the blood separates from the clear liquid in the tube. Not only did John report Jesus' physical signs of death, but also Christ's enemies believed Him to be dead. That was the reason they did not break His legs (John 19:33). Pilate even had the soldiers double check to assure that He was dead.

Another scenario asserted by Muslims is that Jesus never died. Instead, depending on the branch of Islam offering the alternative scenario, someone such as Judas died in His place. Sura 4:157-158 comments on Christ's crucifixion:

> And their saying: Surely we have killed the Messiah, Isa son of Marium, the apostle of Allah; and they did not kill him nor did they crucify him, but it appeared to them so (like Isa) and most surely those who differ therein are only in a doubt about it; they have no knowledge respecting it, but only follow a conjecture, and they killed him not for sure. Nay! Allah took him up to Himself; and Allah is Mighty, Wise.[189]

There are several problems with this view. If Jesus didn't die, who did? There is no evidence or support for Judas dying in Christ's place. Muslims have to suggest that God disguised Jesus so that his own mother didn't recognize Him. Further, the words that Jesus said while on the cross are uncharacteristic for Judas. Jesus asked the Father to forgive His murderers, He offered forgiveness to the thief on the cross beside Him, He gave care of His mother to John, and He committed His spirit into the Father's care. None of these comments would have been made by Judas Iscariot.

John, a man of integrity and Jesus' closest friend, recorded that these were Jesus' comments while hanging on the cross. Not only this, but if Judas had been hanged on the cross, then Judas' body would have been the body in the tomb for everyone to see, and to verify that it was not Jesus Christ.

Thus, Muslims often contend that Jesus did not die at the crucifixion but at a later time. Exactly how this occurred requires conjecture without evidential support. Muslims' rationale for saying that Christ (Isa) did not die stems at least partially from the belief that God would not allow His prophet to die in such a humiliating and dishonorable way. They do agree that Christ was a prophet, albeit a fully human one subordinate to the final prophet, Muhammad. But to deny Christ's humiliation undermines God's chosen means for accomplishing His eternal purpose of salvation. If there had been no sacrificial death, there would be no life for us. And that Jesus died a sacrificial death is exactly what Muslims reject.

Jesus' Corpse Came Back to Life

Since we know miracles are possible, and the authors show evidence of being trustworthy, we can look at the evidence that this historical miracle actually happened. The evidence is comprised of several critical pieces.

First, Jesus' enemies never produced a body, which they would have done immediately if they had a body (see Matt. 28:11-15). Second, there were 12 separate post-resurrection appearances to the women at the tomb, and to disciples, over a period of 40 days, with a total of more than 500 eyewitnesses (see 1 Cor. 15). Jesus ate food, according to Luke 24:42-43, and was touched, according to John 20:27-28. Third, some eyewitnesses who were disbelievers prior to the resurrections became ardent believers because of the resurrection (John 7:1-9, Acts 9:1-19, 1

Cor. 15:1-8). James, Christ's own brother, disbelieved until the resurrection. Others, whose faith was immature, were transformed from hiding cowards to willing martyrs, overnight. Out of the 12 apostles, history records that 11 died martyrs' deaths, never recanting, even under threat of death.

Jehovah's Witnesses argue that Jesus' resurrection was merely spiritual, not physical. Exactly how, though, can a spiritual resurrection be verified? If His resurrection was only spiritual, how would we even *know* He arose, and how do we distinguish between true and false claims of resurrection? Further, though 1 Corinthians 15:44 calls Christ's body a "spiritual body," which Jehovah's Witnesses use to bolster their claim of a spiritual resurrection, apologist Norman Geisler observes that the Greek word for body, "soma," always refers to a physical, rather than a spiritual, body. The resurrected "spiritual" body is immortal, not immaterial. The New Testament uses the word "flesh" four times for Jesus' resurrection body, and Luke notes the disciples' error in thinking they saw a spirit (Luke 24:37).[190]

Lastly, the Jehovah's Witnesses' claim that Jesus' body could not have been physical because the scripture says that flesh and blood cannot enter the kingdom (1Cor. 15:50-52) does not stand, because this passage refers specifically to the *corruptible* mortal body. And as Geisler points out, we die corruptible but are raised incorruptible, even though we are in the same physical body in which we died. Luke 24:39, for instance, describes Jesus Christ's post-resurrection body as flesh and bones, not immaterial.[191]

Could Jesus' disciples have stolen the body? This is exactly the story that the Romans perpetuated. But we have already shown that it is most reasonable to believe that the disciples of Christ were sincere believers in Jesus and men whose characters do not align with the deceptive traits required of someone who would steal and hide the body to promote a myth. Nor could the disciples get past the cohort of Roman soldiers whom Pilate assigned to guard the tomb for exactly the purpose of preventing His body from being stolen. Imagine their rolling the mammoth stone from in front of the tomb while the guards slept.

Maybe all the disciples just hallucinated seeing Christ after the resurrection. This assertion misses the mark by failing to explain how over 500 people witnessed the same thing at 12 different times over 40 days. People don't hallucinate the same thing as groups.

Or, maybe they just went to the wrong tomb. But how did they do this, since John as one of the disciples, knew exactly whose tomb it was? And how did they keep going to the wrong tomb over a period of 40 days?

In summary, several aspects of the resurrection serve as evidence of its reality. Jesus predicted several times that He would die and rise from the dead. The resurrection has more evidential support than any other event in ancient history, being confirmed by nine authors in 27 books during the first century when eyewitnesses still lived. The disciples proclaimed that the tomb was empty. Jesus' enemies never produced a body (Matt. 28:11-15). Christ was seen by (1 Cor. 15:7), touched by (John 20:27-28), and ate food with (Luke 24:42-43) more than 500 eyewitnesses. He appeared in the same physical body, with the same wounds, in which he was buried (John 20-21). Since the physical body dies, it is the physical body that is raised (1 Cor. 15). Finally, the disciples were transformed from scared, skeptical disciples to bold witnesses, most of whom died as martyrs, claiming that Jesus indeed arose (Acts 2). Thousands of unbelievers were converted (Acts 2:41), including many priests (Acts 6:7, 15:5), because of Jesus' resurrection.[192]

23

Did Jesus Confirm the Bible Was God's Word?

We have provided evidence that the New Testament documents are trustworthy, having far greater evidence for their accuracy and authenticity than any other ancient document. We have also provided evidence that Jesus is God in the flesh. With these two truths firmly established, we can now show that in the New Testament, Jesus Himself confirms the truth of the Old Testament. Further, New Testament writers also confirm Christ's promise that the apostles would be enabled by the Holy Spirit to recall what Jesus said and did. We have the written record of those recollections in our New Testament.

Establishing that the Bible is not only reliable but is also God's very Word to mankind is critical, since many religions claim their sacred documents are God's Word. Hindus have the *Bhagavad Gita*, Muslims, the *Qur'an*. Mormons claim their *Book of Mormon* is "another testament of Jesus Christ," and the Catholic Bible includes the *Apocrypha*, believed by Catholics to be inspired.

Does the Bible Claim to Be God's Word?

The question of whether Bible writers claim that the writings are God-breathed (inspired) is significant. As we have noted, a claim that a writing is of divine origin does nothing to prove that it actually is. Still, if there were no internal claim to divine origin, there is no reason that we should attribute divine origin to it.

When we consider whether the Bible is claimed to be inspired by the writers, we have to ask what comprised the Bible in the first-century A.D. Evidently, all 39 books we know as the Old Testament were viewed as the canon of Scripture, although the Jewish people, who were the designated caretakers of God's Word, numbered them differently.

Numerous Old Testament prophets claimed that God spoke through them. For example, in Deuteronomy 18:18 Moses wrote that God said to him, "I will put my words in his mouth." In 2 Samuel 23:2, David said, "The spirit of the LORD spoke though me."

Peter in the New Testament claimed divine origin for the entire Old Testament, those books which comprised the Bible for early Christians in the first century A.D. before the New Testament books were all completed and compiled. He said that biblical writers were "carried along" by the Holy Spirit (2 Pet. 1:20-21). Paul said Scriptures were breathed out by God (2 Tim. 3:16). So, the writers themselves often verbalized their belief that they were writing the words of God. Further, New Testament writers treated specific books as sacred.

As far as how New Testament authors viewed their writings, we see that Paul called Luke's writings "Scripture" in 1 Timothy 5:18. Keep in mind that Luke wrote the largest amount of content in the New Testament. Paul quotes Luke 10:7 as Scripture, holding the same authority as the Old Testament. Peter called Paul's writing Scripture in 2 Peter 3:15-16. Since Paul wrote the most books of the New Testament and Luke wrote the largest amount of content, it is safe to say that these writers believed that the New Testament, as we know it, comprised the words of God to mankind. They treated the words written by other New Testament writers as Scripture, as sacred words to be obeyed and cherished with the same devotion as the Old Testament books.

Did Jesus Confirm the Entire Old Testament as God's Word?

Later in the day of Jesus' resurrection, Luke records that two disciples were making the seven-mile trek from Jerusalem to Emmaus, when Jesus joined them. Not recognizing Him they began to explain the events surrounding the death of a man called Jesus of Nazareth. Jesus listened to their story. Then, Luke 24:27 says that, starting with Moses' and the prophets' writings, Jesus interpreted the Old Testament scriptures that talked about Him. After arriving in Emmaus, as they ate a meal together, they suddenly recognized Him, and He disappeared from their sight.

Immediately, they returned to Jerusalem and found the other disciples, who gathered together, and shared their experiences of seeing the risen Lord. While they were talking, Jesus appeared standing among them. At their shocked response, He assured them that He was not a spirit, but a physical man, inviting them to touch Him. He then ate with them. Then, just before He opened their understanding to receive the truths He would share about Himself from the Old Testament, He prefaced the discussion with a startling claim: "These are my words that I spoke to you while I was still with you, that everything written about me in the Law of Moses and the Prophets and the Psalms must be fulfilled" (Luke 24:44).

In this verse Jesus identified Scripture (God's Word) as consisting of the three sections of the Jewish *TaNaKh*, the exact same Old Testament books we have, but ordered and combined differently. The *Torah* (T) comprised the five books of Moses, also called the Pentateuch. The second section, the Prophets, was called the *Nevi'im* (N) and consisted of five books by the major prophets, and the 12 minor prophets, (the minor prophets' books called "minor" because they were shorter than the major prophets' books). Finally, the third section was called the *Kethubim* (K), or Writings, of which Psalms was the flagship representative book. The Writings included the remaining books such as Esther, Proverbs, and Ecclesiastes.

What is most amazing about Luke 24:44 is the fact that Luke quotes Jesus as asserting that the entire Old Testament—all three sections of the *TaNaKh*—were written about *Him*. Further, the significance of Christ identifying the three sections of the *TaNaKh* means that by the time of Christ in the first century A.D., the canon of the Old Testament was complete, and it was a tripartite (three-part) canon.[193] That is, the Old Testament books that were viewed as sacred were divided into three sections, and they consisted of the same books that comprise our current Old Testament.

Jesus made other specific claims about the Old Testament Scriptures that confirmed His view that they comprised God's own words to mankind. In Matthew 5:18 He claimed that the Scriptures would never perish and "not one jot or tittle," would pass from the Law until all was fulfilled. In Matthew 4 He also affirmed that the Old Testament Scriptures were authoritative by quoting them in response to temptation, repeatedly countering Satan's enticements with, "It is written."

Jesus asserted the trustworthiness of Scripture by affirming that Scripture cannot be broken, in John 10:35. In Matthew 22:29 He chided the teachers of the Law for erring by not knowing the Scripture, an assertion that implied that while the teachers of the law *were* in error, the Scriptures were *not* in error.

Jesus affirmed that the Old Testament was scientifically accurate. Genesis 1-2 affirms that the universe had a beginning and was created by God. These chapters also assert that Adam and Eve were the first humans, and came into existence by direct creation of God. In Matthew 19:4 Jesus responded to the Pharisees' question about divorce by saying, "Have you not read . . .?" He was criticizing the religious leaders who wielded Scripture to entrap Him, while at the same time they displayed ignorance of (or simply denied) foundational scriptural truth. He went on to affirm that Adam and Eve were directly created by God as the first humans (Matt. 19).

Jesus also confirmed the historical accuracy of the Old Testament by speaking of several Old Testament figures as real, historical people. In Matthew 12:40 He asserted that Jonah was a real person who was really in the belly of a fish. Christ also affirmed that Daniel was a prophet who foretold events, rather than a historian who recorded past events. He confirmed that Daniel's prophecy was going to be fulfilled in the future and gave the signs of its fulfillment (Matt. 24:15).

Jesus, then, in His own words, taught that the entire Old Testament, known as the *TaNaKh* to the Jews, was God's very Word to mankind. Further, He claimed that the entire body of Old Testament writings cast Him as the central figure about whom they were written.

Not only did Jesus confirm the Old Testament's divine origin in its entirety, but also Old Testament believers preserved the books they viewed as God's Word. Their chain of custody was as rigorous, if not more so, than the chain of custody presented by J. Warner Wallace for the New Testament. Moses' books were immediately viewed by Israel as holy, according to Deuteronomy 31:26. Joshua's writings were placed with Moses's Law, according to Joshua 24:26. The prophet Samuel added to the library, according to 1 Samuel 10:25. Daniel viewed Jeremiah's writing and the Law as sacred, according to Daniel 9:2, 11, and 13. Every book pointed toward the Messiah.[194]

Did Jesus Say the New Testament Would Be Written?

It may seem odd to ask if Jesus said anything about the New Testament, given the fact that it wasn't yet written in His lifetime. But He did, in fact, verbally forecast the writing of His words and deeds, which is exactly what the Gospel writers did. Observe the sequence of sayings and events that Geisler and Turek identify in the development of the New Testament documents.

Jesus was the full and final revelation of God as the Messiah, according to Colossians 2:9. He commissioned 12 apostles, promising the Spirit would guide them into all truth and remind them of all He had said and done, according to John 14:26.

The early church was built on the foundation of the apostles and prophets, according to Ephesians 2:20. Acts 2:42 explains that after Peter's message, when more than 3,000 persons were saved, the growing church continued following the apostles' teachings. These apostles lived and died in the first century during the era of the eyewitnesses and were verified by miracles. The only authentic record of their teachings is the New Testament.

Later, when heresies threatened, the Church formalized the canon at the church councils. These councils did not determine sacred Scripture but discovered and formalized what Jewish believers and the early church had *already* recognized as sacred.[195]

Why Do Evangelicals Reject the Apocrypha & Gnostic Gospels?

The *Apocrypha* consists of 11-12 extra writings, seven extra books and four extra writings in Esther/Daniel. Catholics accept these books as sacred. Protestants do not. There are several critical reasons why we as Christian evangelicals do not accept these writings as Scripture.[196]

None of the writings claims to be prophetic, as did many of the Old Testament books. In fact, I Maccabees 9:27 clearly claims it is not. Nor did prophets write any of these books, the prophetic era ceasing in the fourth century B.C. Further, none contains any prophetic predictions that characterize the Old Testament books and serve as authenticating verification that they are true.

Romans 3:2 says that to the Jews were entrusted "the oracles of God." The Jewish people, then, were the custodians of God's Word. The Jewish people have never accepted as Scripture these books, nor did Jesus or His apostles ever quote them as authoritative Scripture. This is significant because it is clear from Scripture that they knew these books existed, and may have alluded to them (Heb. 11:35 may allude to 2 Maccabees 7, 12). In contrast, the New Testament quotes Old Testament passages hundreds of times.

None of these books were accepted by the early church. Though Catholics as a whole accept the *Apocrypha* as Scripture, the famous Catholic scholar, Jerome, rejected them. Finally, these writings contain false teachings, and thus, they cannot be God's Word. For example, they affirm intercessory prayer for the dead and purgatory.[197]

One last word needs to be said about another group of writings sometimes asserted to be inspired by God. The Gnostic Gospels (*Nag Hammadi*) often bear the names of apostles or eyewitnesses. However, we know that they cannot be written by the apostles for one simple reason. They appeared a century *after* the New Testament Gospels. Since they were not written in the eyewitness era, they cannot be of divine origin.[198]

Final Thoughts

There is so much more that could be said about the foundational evidences for our Christian faith. There are not enough volumes in the world to contain the evidence. Nevertheless, the evidence we have shared here is more than sufficient to establish that Christianity is the most logical and reasonable explanation of reality. Most importantly, the evidence shows that not only does objective truth exist, not only does God exist, but also that God has personally entered our world as Jesus Christ. He has confirmed to us that the Old and New Testaments speak the truth and reveal to us all that God would have us know in order to receive forgiveness and restore a right relationship with our Maker.

Part 5

Talk to Walk Them to the Gospel

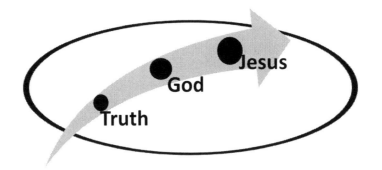

24

Preparing Ourselves for the Task Before Us

We have spent the bulk of this book talking about *what* to say to people about Christianity. The *content* of our message is the evidence supporting Christianity's truth claims, claims about the existence of truth, God, miracles, New Testament reliability, as well as the evidence that Jesus is really God in the flesh.

Sadly, it is possible to have a wealth of knowledge far beyond what we have talked about here and still crash and burn in a conversation. This is because *what* we need to say isn't the whole story. We need to know *how* to say it, as well. We need to learn how to talk to people in such a way as to walk them to the gospel. There are several things we can do to make our conversation redemption focused, so we don't get on a merry-go-round of words that goes nowhere.

Evaluate Whether You Are in the Faith

In order to share our faith, we must be *in* the faith. Paul urged the Corinthian church members to examine themselves on the basis of Christ's requirements, to see if they were truly believers. "Examine yourselves, to see whether you are in the faith. Test yourselves. Or do you not realize this about yourselves, that Jesus Christ is in you?—unless indeed you fail to meet the test!" (2 Cor. 13:5). If statistics are correct in saying that large numbers of lost people fill the membership rolls of our churches, then it's time to clearly distinguish between true faith—a faith that saves, and faux faith—a vacuous form of godliness.

A person with **true faith** reflects the following characteristics:

*She has godly sorrow over her sin that produces repentance (2 Cor. 7:10).
*She has a testimony of conversion (John 3:3).
*She has received salvation at the moment of repentance and faith (Rom. 10:13).
*She is saved on the basis of God's grace through faith alone (Eph. 2:8-10).
*She has committed her life to Jesus Christ, God in the flesh (Luke 9:23, John 1:14).
*She has a transformed heart (Gal. 2:20).
*She reflects faith through transformed actions as a "doer" of the Word (James 2:22).
*She is enabled to discern God's will (1 Cor. 2:14-15).
*She trusts Jesus as the only way to salvation (John 14:6).
*She believes that Jesus Christ was raised and lives today (Rom. 10:9-10).
*She has the witness of the Holy Spirit within (Rom. 8:16).

A person with **faux faith** exhibits the following attributes:

*She may experience regret without repentance toward God (2 Cor. 7:8).
*She may believe that she has gradually grown into salvation (John 3:3).
*She may believe that she must be morally good (or work) in addition to displaying faith for salvation (Gal. 3:1-3).
*She may believe in God, without believing in the one whom He sent (James 2:19, John 6:29).
*She may mentally agree with the fact that Jesus lived and died for her sins.
*She may be very religious or very spiritual (2 Tim 3:5, 7).
*She may believe Jesus is *a* way to salvation (John 14:6, Acts 4:12).
*She has no transformed heart, and possesses no ability to please God or to discern His will (1 Cor. 2:14).
*She has no power of the indwelling Holy Spirit (1 Cor. 6:19).
*She may believe she is saved at least partially because she is a good person who tries to do good things (Eph. 2:8-9).[199]

Since conversion by definition involves change, we must ask ourselves whether the Lord Jesus has changed us. I was very young when I trusted Christ as Savior, but I still struggle against enough sinful attitudes and habits to imagine what my life would be like had He not saved me. Not only would I be at my worst—I would be without hope in utter despair. That thought alone makes me wonder how people survive life's crises without Jesus.

If you harbor any doubts about your relationship with Jesus Christ and your eternal destination, do not allow anything to stop you from coming to Jesus, even if you have long thought you were a Christian, even if you hold an honored position as a Christian leader in your church, even if you have taught Sunday school, or even if you have witnessed to others. A guide for responding in faith to Jesus is provided in this book just for you.

I myself struggled as a teen, wondering if my decision as a child to accept Jesus was sincere, and if I had understood enough to be saved. I was embarrassed that I had told others how to receive Christ as Savior and yet experienced doubts myself. Finally, I talked with my parents, settled the issue, and nailed it down.

A dear ordained minister friend of mine also one day realized he had walked down the aisle as a child, but had never personally asked Jesus Christ to be His Savior. He trusted Jesus and made a public profession of faith, even though some folks who had always thought of him as a Christian felt uncomfortable.

Friend, if you are in the same boat, I urge you: Don't test God's patience. I ask the Lord now to give you the courage, humility, and sense of urgency to fall on your knees, repent of your sin, and invite Jesus to be your personal Savior.[200]

Share Reasons in the Context of Relationship

Once our personal relationship with Christ is settled, we can then prepare ourselves to engage others in redemptive conversations. In his book, *The Master Plan of Evangelism*, author Robert E. Coleman says that one of Jesus' main strategies for teaching His disciples how to share the gospel was simply "being with them."[201] The basic, yet profound, truth of this assertion is that if we want to love people, teach them, and yes, to share the gospel with them, we must be *with* them. What is true for discipleship, is also true for evangelism and pre-evangelism, which is apologetics.

So often we expect to present all the evidence in rapid-fire bullet points and elicit a response from the skeptic. But apologetics is not for the faint of heart. Transformation most often occurs in the context of relationship. The very fact that we do not give up on the friend who mocks our faith, challenges every assertion about the truth of Christianity, and wholly rejects our efforts to help her understand, can be the most powerful witness. We are urged in Scripture not to give up. Paul says, "Let us not grow weary of doing good, for in due season we will reap, if we do not give up" (Gal. 6:9).

We can intentionally develop relationships with women in our own age group. In addition, we can initiate mentoring relationships with younger women, providing support and encouragement to those coming along behind us. In the context of these trusting relationships, we will find that opportunities to share our faith will arise naturally.[202]

Keep the Central Goal in View

The only way to keep from growing weary in the sense of yielding to frustration and disillusionment is to keep in view a biblical motivation and goal. If we were to ask ourselves what Jesus' motivation was for ministering to people, we may be tempted to say that He wanted to meet their needs. But, while His secondary goal was to meet people's needs, that was not His primary goal. Nor will the desire to meet people's needs sustain *us* in ministry. The reality is that the needs of people will always exceed our ability to meet those needs.

Further, whenever our motivating goal is to meet needs, we can become discouraged and even angry when people reject our efforts, or when we do not meet our self-designed goals. I recognized this on a mission trip to Zimbabwe in the 1980s. Volunteers who came to dig water wells often left a few weeks later with nothing to show for their efforts. They spent the majority of their trip ordering and waiting on parts, which often arrived only after the volunteers had returned home. Such is life in Africa.

We can change our goal from a temporal focus to a kingdom focus. And we can do this daily. Jesus revealed the key to His success: "My food is to do the will of Him who sent Me, and to accomplish His work" (John 4:34). When "we make it our aim to please Him" (2 Cor. 5:9), we are freed from measuring success by people's responses. Jesus looked to the Father's face, not to the faces of humans, for affirmation: "But Jesus, on His part, was not entrusting Himself to them, for He knew all men, and because He did not need anyone to bear witness concerning man, for He Himself knew what was in man" (John 2:24-25). And because Jesus looked to please the Father, He was able to say at the end of His life: "I glorified you on earth, having accomplished the work that you gave me to do" (John 17:4).

Our goal is to obey the Lord by speaking the truth. We are not responsible for the way people respond. Luke recounts in Acts 28 how Paul, after arriving in Rome, was given the opportunity to share the evidence of Christ's identity with Jewish leaders. Luke says that Paul poured his heart out all day long: "From morning till evening he expounded to them, testifying to the kingdom of God and trying to convince them about Jesus both from the Law of Moses and from the Prophets." The results? "And some were convinced by what he said, but others disbelieved" (Acts 28:25). Our story will be the same. Some will believe and some won't. Either way we have succeeded when we do all to the glory of Jesus.

Ask the Holy Spirit for Help

The quickest way to fail before we ever get started in the apologetics endeavor is to do it in our own strength. My greatest weakness is just this. I simply start moving forward and in my zeal, fail to talk with the Lord and ask for His help, or to submit my plans to His.

We are to share the truth, recognizing it is the Spirit who uses it to convince people of their sinfulness in light of Christ's righteousness. "And when he comes, he will convict the world concerning sin and righteousness and judgment" (John 16:8). We can never underestimate the power of the Holy Spirit in turning the ready heart toward God.

How many Christians who lived in Paul's day would ever have imagined that Saul, later called Paul, would turn to faith in Christ as he walked the road to Damascus for the express purpose of persecuting Christians? None. In fact, even after he had trusted Christ, he had to have Barnabas verify that his conversion was genuine (Acts 9:27), because the disciples feared him. But the Spirit changed Paul's heart. And the Spirit changes hearts today. So, we share and trust the results to Him.

Be Patient with People

After reading all the evidences in this book, we may be tempted to give up. The volume of information is overwhelming, and the task is just too big. We feel paralyzed. We think, *I'll never be able to answer all of someone's questions or remember which evidence to share in response to a specific objection.* These are common fears that run through our minds as we think about actually talking to someone about evidences for the truth of Christianity.

During my years as a high school apologetics teacher, I often gave an assignment to students that required them to engage in a conversation with a skeptic or person who held a different worldview than theirs. Frequently, students returned from conversations saying, "They had an answers for all my arguments." Perhaps they expected that the skeptic would raise a question, they as Christians would present evidence or a counter argument, and then the skeptic would say, "Aha! Now I understand," and change her mind immediately. Most conversations don't work that way.

I have often reassured myself after a difficult conversation, that regardless of how a person responds, my love for her and the truths I've shared will be replayed the moment she lays her head on the pillow at night. A change of mind often occurs after a time of reflection. But whether or not the skeptic does change her mind, I need to remember to love her as Christ loves her, and to share the truths that bring life.

Put Your Emotions in Their Place

It is normal to feel anxiety when we take risks in spiritual conversations. But we do have a choice as to how we will respond to our emotions. By nature, I am a very tense and intense person. I have struggled with anxiety my entire life. Feeling guilty about our emotional make up and tendencies isn't helpful.

One strategy we can practice for putting our emotions in their place is to continuously remove ourselves from the center stage of our heart and place the Lord there. We focus our thoughts on His honor, His glory, and His fame. First Peter 3:15 explains that this is how we make ourselves ready to offer a defense of the gospel: "In your hearts honor Christ the Lord as holy," which the NKJV words as "sanctify the Lord God in your hearts."

The second calming strategy that we can practice is to love people instead of looking at them as a threat or as someone to defeat. Their souls are at stake. God has called and equipped us as lifegiving vessels. It is a difficult, but holy, calling.

25

Cultivating Core Conversations

Think about people you care about who are unbelievers or who have questions about Christianity's truth claims. We want to engage them in what I call "core conversations." Core conversations are interactions that address the core issues of life, the things that really matter. They touch upon the big questions of life, such as origin, identity, meaning, knowledge, morality, and destiny, which we studied earlier.

As mentioned, we can have all the information we need to answer the skeptic's questions and still falter in a dialogue. In working with students I found that taking the knowledge into a conversation and sharing in a helpful, redemptive way is one of the toughest aspects of doing apologetics. The transition from theory to practice is challenging.

Conversations seldom progress logically from one topic to another as presented in this book. More often they are messy and convoluted. For this reason, we need to practice and develop skills in navigating conversations in a way that truly helps the listener and moves the conversation toward the saving gospel of Jesus Christ. Things we need to learn include listening for clues to the core issues troubling the skeptic, developing the ability to respond with confidence, gentleness, and respect instead of defensiveness, mastering basic communication strategies that yield mutual understanding, and honing the ability to direct and pace the conversation.

Engage with the "Presenting Problem"

When a patient comes to a health care provider, the physician or nurse practitioner first listens to the patient share the problem that led to her making an appointment. The presenting problem is the starting point of the conversation. While it is true there may be an underlying issue not yet identified, we have to start somewhere, and listening carefully to what the individual *sees* as her problem, and responding to her verbalized need, builds the trust that will be needed later for her to invest and participate in the health care provider's treatment plan.

When we find ourselves in day-to-day conversations with friends, co-workers, and family members, they often, like us, share problems they are facing. If the individual is struggling with a crisis, the problem itself provides a great open door for bringing up spiritual matters. We might say something like, "Where do you find strength to deal with problems like this?" When we ask this question, we need to listen carefully to her answer. Her answer will enable us to learn how she usually responds to problems, what resources she usually accesses, and what her spiritual concerns are.

We can share how Christ makes a difference for us personally in how we deal with problems and affirm the hope that He brings to every crisis. This personal testimony can be very helpful. Sometimes the person will ask more questions, and we can share the gospel. If, however, she says something like, "Whatever works for you is good," or, "Well, I'm not all that into religion," is the conversation over? No. This is where apologetics is helpful.

Shine the Spotlight on Unspoken Assumptions

An assumption is something we believe to be true that is embedded in our argument, but is usually not stated. It is something we *pre*suppose as true that must be so in order for the verbalized argument to be true. Everyone has assumptions, and they are not necessarily a bad thing. We just need to shine the spotlight on them so that we can evaluate whether they are reasonable and true.

Let's take a look at the skeptic response to our testimony in the previous paragraph. She responded, "Whatever works for you is good." To shine the light on the unspoken assumption in that statement, we might say, "Are you saying that truth is defined as what works for someone?" Listen to her answer. Just exposing the assumption may be enough to help her rethink her comment. We can also offer counterexamples of some things that work that aren't necessarily true. For instance, a person may develop a plausible but false storyline that allows her to avoid conviction of a crime. While the storyline is false, it *works* for her. Does that make it good or true? Challenging assumptions enables us to help the skeptic rethink the reasonableness of her belief. To move forward in the discussion, we may then explain the correspondence view of truth and provide examples of how all people live according to that view in their day-to-day lives.

We also need to shine the light on our own assumptions. When we say, "Homosexuality is wrong because it is unnatural," we can expect for someone to expose our assumption that anything that is unnatural is morally wrong. The skeptic will likely bring up the fact that for amputees a prosthesis is unnatural, but no one thinks that using a prosthesis is morally wrong. One response is to point out that a prosthesis, like many unnatural things, such as eyeglasses for poor vision, serve to restore the natural condition. There are other responses that address the meaning of the "nature" of things, but the point here is that we all have assumptions and need to shine the light on them, so we can evaluate whether these assumptions correspond to reality.

Use Common Ground Redemptively

Apologist Chuck Colson shares a story that illustrates the right way to find and build on common ground with skeptics, to walk them to the gospel. He says that "a well-known media figure," whom he called "Tom," invited him to dinner at a restaurant, specifically to talk about God. Right away Tom said he didn't believe in God, but was open to Chuck's views. Chuck tried several avenues of approach. He shared his testimony, but Tom cut him off, saying that it was fine if Christianity worked for Chuck, but for another friend, crystals worked. Chuck took a different approach, talking with Tom about health problems that Tom had experienced and the inevitability of death. Tom made clear that he believed people were just higher animal forms, and there was no afterlife. Chuck moved to discuss Scripture, but Tom quickly stopped him, saying the Bible was just a fable. Chuck even shared evidences that the Bible was historically reliable, but Tom didn't bite.

Finally, Chuck asked Tom if he had seen Woody Allen's movie, *Crimes and Misdemeanors*, a story about a man who hired a killer to murder his mistress and later was overwhelmed by guilt. Ultimately, the protagonist stifled his guilt with the idea that since we were all just animals anyway, there really was no such thing as justice, right, or wrong.

Chuck challenged Tom to ask himself if he really believed that life was just a matter of stifling guilt or reconciling ourselves to the fact that we are just animals, as Darwin said, and as the movie character believed. Bringing up a movie they had both seen provided the connection Chuck needed in order to introduce Tolstoy's and C.S. Lewis' thoughts on morality, which then led to his sharing the discussion on human conscience, found in Romans 2.

Colson ends the story by saying that God can work any way He wishes. He doesn't need a Woody Allen movie to make a connection with people. But, in this case, that is exactly what the Holy Spirit used to open a door to Tom's heart. "Without Woody Allen, Tolstoy, and C. S. Lewis, I would never have found common ground to discuss spiritual matters." This is an example of how to effectively find and use common ground to walk someone to the gospel.[203]

When seeking common ground, we want to be careful not to compromise our faith. We don't have to capitulate to false assertions. The new tolerance says we must accept as valid all other views that oppose our own. But tolerance presupposes that there is a real difference of opinion; otherwise, there would be nothing to tolerate. We don't agree with the person's worldview and convictions. Nor does she agree with us. That's the whole reason we have a conversation that focuses on truth, not merely commonalities.

We do, however, hold a great deal in common with all other humans: the fundamental first principles of logic/thought; common life experiences, including hopes, dreams, sorrows, griefs, and fears; and often, our culture and language. We can use these touchpoints to meet a person where she is and build a bridge to the truth.

Practice Focused Listening

It is clear from Scripture that we are to focus on listening more than speaking. James says, "Know this, my beloved brothers: let every person be quick to hear, slow to speak, slow to anger; for the anger of man does not produce the righteousness of God" (1:19-20). It is very easy to get sidetracked by anger at the idolatrous views of skeptics. We often jump in, trying to make our points, but would do a better job by just stopping to listen.

Listening also earns us the right to be heard. When we are in conversation with someone who will not allow us to finish a sentence, we can slow the conversation by saying something like, "I want to respond to your questions, but can't do that if I am not able to complete a thought. How about you tell me what you're thinking, and I will listen. Then, I know you will give me the same time and will listen to what I have to say. That way, we will both be heard, and I can answer your questions as you have asked."

Here are a few principles for practicing effective and focused listening:

* Look at the person in the eyes. This demonstrates your respect and willingness to listen.
* Keep your body posture open, avoiding folding your arms over your chest in a defensive mode.
* Lean forward into the conversation, instead of leaning back in an all-knowing, authoritative position.
* Wait for the person to complete a thought without interrupting to express your own ideas.
* Breathe. Whenever I am feeling tense and evaluate my breathing pattern, I often notice I have been unconsciously holding my breath. Just concentrating on breathing helps to diminish the tension.
*Think about what the person is saying, rather than what you are going to say in response.
*Offer signals of affirmation, not necessarily that you agree, but that you are listening, such as a nod or, "I see," or "Go on."

When you do respond:

* Modulate the tone, volume, and pace of your voice.
* Seek to be clear, not intimidating.
* Be direct and honest.
* Ask for feedback to make sure you are understood. [204]

Use Effective Communication Tools

Communication is a two-way street. Let's not forget this simple truth. Just getting everything we know out on the table is not our goal, or at least, it shouldn't be. In order to pace ourselves, listen well, and respond in a helpful way, we can learn how to use specific communication tools.

We want to use these tools to help us understand what the other person is saying and what she means, help her think through the process by which she came to these beliefs, and reveal the ramifications of her beliefs, since beliefs are always based on presuppositions and result in other consequences when taken to their logical conclusions. In the big picture, genuine communication yields understanding and helps us guide the conversation toward the gospel message and an encounter with the person of Jesus Christ.

The tools that I list below are well-known by many communicators. I learned many of these strategies in nursing school, where we as students were actually graded on how effectively we employed communication techniques. Other tools are presented by Greg Koukl, author of *Tactics in Defending the Faith*, who is a master at employing helpful questions to advance the conversation where we want it to go. You will want to check out his resources. His motto is, "Never make an assertion when a question will do."

I have renamed and reframed the tools to rhyme so that they are easy to remember.

1. Verify:

This is a well-known communication technique known as a reflection. You want to make sure you understand what the other person is saying by reflecting back to her what you think she said. You may be surprised how many times you miss what the person was actually trying to communicate. When a friend says, "I don't believe a good God can exist and allow all this evil," you might say, "Let me make sure I understand. You are saying that God cannot exist if evil is in the world because if He did exist He would stop evil. Is that right?" Reframing and reflecting back a person's comment also allows her to hear and evaluate her own assertions.

Imagine a friend says, "I don't believe the New Testament since it could just be a bunch of made up stories." You might verify by saying something like, "So, you are saying that the reason you don't believe that the New Testament speaks the truth is that it is possible that the stories within it are created rather than being a record of actual events?" Taking time to verify also slows down the conversation so that you and the other person both have time to thinks things through. This enables you to respond, not merely to react.

2. Clarify:

Ask what she means by what she said. When she says, "I believe in evolution," you want to know what she means by "evolution." The conversation might go like this:

"What do you mean by the word 'evolution'"?

"I mean change over time. Everything changes over time."

"Yes, I agree with that. But it seems to me you are talking about a specific kind of change. What kind of change are you talking about?"

One point to remember. Thoughtlessly and repeatedly asking, "What do you mean by that?" can be annoying. Don't just use the question as a filler. When you ask, listen carefully to what the person answers. Then seek to clarify or amplify the person's answer.

3. Amplify:

Once you understand what the person is trying to say, then you want to understand the thought process that led to the belief. You might ask, "How did you come to this view?" In other words, what is the evidence or reasoning that resulted in the view she now holds? It is possible she believes that God is everything in the world because she was reared in a Hindu home. As you listen for the reasons the person has come to hold a certain view, you may note inconsistencies or invalid reasons for belief and help her raise questions about the view, as well. You may then draw to her attention the inconsistencies in her view.

After asking the friend in the previous question what she means by "evolution," she says, "Science has proved that all living things came from a single cell." When she makes such an assertion, it is reasonable to ask her to explain or "amplify" how she came to this conclusion.

4. Ramify:

Every view, when taken to its logical end, has ramifications or consequences. *If* a person believes that an all-good, all-powerful God cannot exist because evil is in the world, one of the ramifications of that belief is that she must *then* explain how evil came about in her own view. You might ask, "Have you considered that if evil exists, good exists. And if a real, objective good exists, then a Supreme, Good Being must exist, since things like rocks, not being moral creatures, cannot produce "good" nor "bad"?

Or, you might say, "Given the fact that you don't believe there is a God, how do you explain where good and evil came from?" In asking this question, as Turek pointed out in the chapter on evil, we are not saying that atheists can't live good, moral lives. We are observing the reality that even though they may live good, moral lives, they have no good reason to do so, given their own worldview that good and evil are just created by human personal opinion. While employing this type of probing requires us to build some background knowledge, we have already learned enough from this book to start using this tool.

26

Sharing the Gospel Message

Our sole aim in this book is to walk the skeptic to this point in the conversation: preparing the heart to receive the gospel of Jesus Christ. We have provided ample evidence for Christianity's truth claims about Jesus. If truth exists, if it is true that God is the Creator who made us for relationship with Him, if God has revealed Himself through miracles, if the New Testament is a reliable document, if in this New Testament Jesus claimed and proved Himself to be God, and if as God, Jesus Himself affirmed that the Bible is the very Word of God to us, then Jesus Christ is worthy of our worship, He is the rightful owner of our lives, and He is our only hope for restoring our relationship with God that has been broken by our sin.

We can share with someone how to trust Jesus Christ as her Savior. We begin by sharing who God is and what His plan is for humans. We then explain how all of us as humans have rebelled against God and how our sin separates us from God. Then, we talk about the remedy for our sin provided through Jesus Christ's sacrificial death in our place, and His victory over death and sin by His resurrection from the dead. Finally, we invite the person to believe in—to trust—Jesus Christ as her personal Savior. When she receives God's free gift of forgiveness, salvation, and eternal life through faith in Christ, peace is restored in her relationship with God.

If you have realized as you read this book that you are not a believer, but would like to be, this message is also for you. There is no greater joy than realizing that we have a need that can be completely filled by God. Look up the scriptures in a Bible as you go along. It is the truth of God's Word that reveals how we can restore our relationship with Him.

The Plan: Created for Relationship with God

Scripture says that God is the holy Creator. He created us in His own image for relationship with Him (Gen. 2, Col .1:16, Psalm 139). God loves us and desires the best for you and me. *He* is our best (Eph. 5:2, John 3:16).

The Problem: Our Sin

Scripture explains that all humans have sinned, being sinners by nature and by choice (Rom. 3:10, 3:23). Sin is thinking and acting as the boss of ourselves, against God. Think of a target with a bullseye on it. When we shoot our arrows, we try to hit the bullseye, but we consistently miss the mark. Sin is like that. We want to do good, but we find we always fall short. Adam and Eve sinned when they disobeyed God in Genesis 3, and every human has followed in their steps since creation (Rom. 5:12, Isa. 53:6).

Being holy, God cannot ignore sin. If He did not judge sin as evil, then He would not be a holy God (Isa. 5:16). Since God *is* holy, sin separates us from Him. The Scripture calls this separation "death." "Death" in the Bible means both physical separation of the soul from body and also spiritual separation of the soul from God (Rom. 6:23, Isa. 59:2). The Bible says that in our natural state we are enemies of God (Rom. 5:10). As enemies, we cannot make things right by doing "good" things (Isa. 64:6).

The Provision: Jesus' Death and Resurrection on Our Behalf

God from eternity had already planned the remedy for our sin. As our Creator, He alone can fix our sin problem. He can forgive us, give us new life, and provide us with hope (Rom. 8:3-4, 1 Pet. 1:18-19). God sent His Son, Jesus Christ, to live the perfect life we couldn't live and to pay the penalty for our sin, dying and taking the punishment for our sin, in our place, so we wouldn't have to be separated from God. Death was not the end for Jesus. Three days after He was buried, He physically rose from the dead, victorious over sin and death. He promises us this same resurrection and eternal life, as well (Rom. 5:8, 6:4, 10:9-10).

The Point of Decision: Believe and Receive

If we agree with God about our sinfulness, and want to turn from our sin in repentance to trust in Jesus to forgive us, He will restore our relationship with God (Rom. 10:9-10, 1 John 1:9-10). Through faith in the work of Christ alone (not any good work that we could ever do), we can be saved. Jesus promised that when we trust Him, the Holy Spirit enters our life, guides us into truth, and gives us power over sin (2 Cor. 5:17, Gal. 5:16). We become a child of God (John 1:12). He also promised that He will never leave or forsake us (Heb. 13:5). When we die, Jesus promised that we will have eternal life with Him (John 3:16).

To ask for the free gift of forgiveness and salvation, we can say:

Jesus, I am a sinner and I cannot fix my sin problem. Thank you for coming to earth as God in the flesh and paying the penalty for my sin. I trust You to forgive my sin, live in my life, and give me the sure hope of heaven. Amen.

There is nothing magical in the words of this prayer. It is our heart's decision that changes us from an enemy of God to becoming God's child forever. If the request for salvation is sincere, the transformation is complete and final. The transformation may be accompanied by tears; it may not. It may be accompanied by an immediate awareness of God's peace; it may not. It is not our emotional response that assures us that we are saved. Rather, we know we are saved because we trust that God has kept all of His promises thus far, and will keep His promise to save all who call upon Jesus for salvation.

We never need to worry about losing our relationship with God. It is Christ's work that keeps us saved, not our ability to do what is right. We will fail many times. But He promises never to leave us or forsake us.

There are several steps we can take as a new believer to strengthen our faith and begin to mature in Christ. Getting a Bible so that we can start a daily reading plan immediately is critical. There are numerous Bible reading plans online. Reading through the Gospels is a great place to start. Talking with God through prayer each day is also an integral part of building this new relationship. God desires to be known by us, so it is important to use the tools of prayer and the Bible to do so.

Getting connected to a good church that teaches the truth about the Bible is one of the most important things we can do as new believers. We can ask the Lord to guide us to a church home, where we can learn and mature as believers in Christ. We can read a church's statement of faith online to assure it teaches the truth.

Conclusion

We have covered a lot of territory in our time together. I pray that though you may feel you've been fed from a firehose and your brain feels like mush, that you will not give up. I pray that you will relentlessly pursue understanding and sharing with others the evidences undergirding our faith. The best way to remember what you've learned is to practice sharing it. When you do forget, and we all do, simply go back to your resources and read again.

Pursuing knowing God is a worthwhile and lifelong journey, one in which we never truly "arrive." This is as it should be, for the Lord continues throughout our lives to complete the good work He has begun in us.

Lord Jesus, we thank you for this opportunity to learn together. You are so good to provide us with this world, through which Your creative and sustaining hand is evident in every place. We need you and trust you to help us recall all we have learned. We ask you to help us use this knowledge wisely, not to become puffed up, but to bring people to you and to strengthen the faith of believers. To you, precious Savior, be all glory and honor, forever.

If you have questions or would like to share with me a decision, please email me at **triciaspeaks@yahoo.com**. I also would love to hear about your experiences in sharing the reasons for the hope within.

Love in Christ,

Tricia

Endnotes

1. "Interview with Daniel B. Wallace On Textual Criticism," Bible.org.

2. John Argubright, "To the Unknown God," Biblehistory.com, 2013.

3. Bill and Anabel Gillham, *Victorious Christian Living* audiocassette album (Springfield: Grace Friendship, 1981).

4. Norman L. Geisler, *Baker Encyclopedia of Christian Apologetics* (Grand Rapids, MI: Baker Academic, 1999), 741.

5. Walter Truett Anderson, *Reality Isn't What It Used to Be: Theatrical Politics, Ready-to-wear Religion, Global Myths, Primitive Chic, and Other Wonders of the Postmodern World* (HarperCollins Ebooks).

6. Jim Pryor, "Philosophical Terms and Methods."

7. Geisler, 703.

8. Ibid.

9. J.P. Moreland, "What Are Self-Defeating Statements?" From Hooligan to Accountant, January 17, 2012.

10. "Can Science Alone Answer Our Questions? Peter Atkins Talks to Stephen Law," Humanists4Science, April 2, 2007.

11. Thomas Howe, *Objectivity in Biblical Interpretation*, (n.p: Advantage Inspirational, 2005), Norman Geisler under "Foreword."

12. Thomas Howe, *Objectivity in Biblical Interpretation* (n.p.: Advantage Inspirational, 2005).

13. Moreland.

14. Ibid.

15. Richard Dawkins, *River Out of Eden: A Darwinian View of Life* (New York: Basic Books, 1995), 133.

16. Ronald H. Nash, *The Gospel and the Greeks: Did the New Testament Borrow from Pagan Thought?* 2nd ed. (Phillipsburg, NJ: P & R Publishing, 2003), 6.

17. Ibid.

18. A.W. Tozer, *Knowledge of the Holy* (n.p.: Lulu Press, 2013), 3.

19. Norman L. Geisler, *Christian Apologetics*, 2nd ed. (Grand Rapids: Baker Academic, 2013), under "Preface."

20. Frank Turek, "Is Atheism a Lack of Belief in God?" crossexamined.org, July 19, 2014.

21. Richard Howe, "New Atheism," National Conference on Christian Apologetics, conference notes, 2013. I am not certain of this date, and Richard has made this comment in numerous presentations, including seminary classes in which I have been a student.

22. Peter Kreeft, "The First Cause Argument," peterkreeft.com.

23. Hugh Ross, "Quantum Mechanics," Reasons to Believe, January 1, 2009.

24. Lawrence Krauss, "A Universe from Nothing" (video), 2009.

25. Ibid.

26. Hugh Ross, "A Universe from Nothing? A Critique of Lawrence Krauss' Book, Part 1," Reasons to Believe, April 9, 2012.

27. Ibid.

28. David Albert, "On the Origin of Everything: Sunday Review: A Universe from Nothing," review, New York Times, March 23, 2012.

29. Janna Levin, "Big Bang Briefly (Ep. 1)," (video).

30. Nola Taylor Redd, "Einstein's Theory of General Relativity," space.com, July 12, 2016.

31. Ibid.

32. Ibid.

33. Sten Odenwald, "Special and General Relativity Questions and Answers: Can Space Exist Without Matter and Energy Around?" Gravity Probe B: NASA Astronomy Cafe, accessed September 25, 2016.

34. Einstein Online. "Reddening Galaxies." Accessed August 25, 2016.

35. Prem Isaac, "Why the Point of Singularity Count Not Have Been Eternal," Personal communication, February 13, 2011.

36. Jim Lucas, "What Is the Second Law of Thermodynamics," Live Science, May 22, 2015, www.livescience.com.

37. Ibid.

38. "Pick-up Sticks," Wikipedia.

39. Lucas.

40. Henry M. Morris, "Does Entropy Contradict Evolution," The Institute for Creation Research, 1985.

41. Lucas.

42. "Bacteria," Microbiology Online.

43. Josh Rosenau, "Historical Science vs. Experimental Science," National Center for Science Education, September 24, 2008.

44. Ibid.

45. William Dembski, "If Only Darwinists Scrutinized Their Own Work as Closely: A Response to 'Erik,'" billdembski.com.

46. Richard Dawkins, *The Blind Watchmaker: Why the Evidence of Evolution Reveals a Universe Without Design* (New York: W.W. Norton and Company, 1986), 21.

47. Hugh Ross, "Design and the Anthropic Principle," Reasons to Believe, January 1, 1989.

48. Ibid.

49. Ibid.

50. William Dembski, "Why Natural Selection Cannot Design Anything," Association of Christians in the Mathematical Sciences, 2001.

51. William Dembski, "Detecting Design by Eliminating Chance: A Response to Robin Collins," 11, billdembski.com.

52. "What Is a Genome?" Genetics Home Reference: U.S. National Library of Medicine.

53. Francis S. Collins, *The Language of God: A Scientist Presents Evidence for Belief* (New York: Free Press, 2006), 102-103.

54. "Do All Cells Have the Same DNA? 2009 National DNA Day Chatroom Transcript," NIH: National Human Genome Research Institute.

55. Thomas Woodward and James P. Gills, *The Mysterious Epigenome: What Lies Beyond DNA* (Grand Rapids: Kregel, 2012), 9.

56. Thomas Woodward, "The Mysterious Epigenome: What Lies Behind DNA" (podcast), December 4, 2015, 4:44.

57. Woodward and Gills, 15.

58. "How Do Flashlights Work?"

59. Michael J. Behe, *Darwin's Black Box: The Biochemical Challenge to Evolution* (New York: Free Press, 2006), 5.

60. Ibid., 64-65.

61. Ibid., 65.

62. Ibid., 66.

63. Ibid., 67.

64. J.L. Mackie, *The Miracle of Theism: Arguments for and Against the Existence of God* (Oxford: Oxford University Press, 1982), 15.

65. C.S. Lewis, *Mere Christianity* (New York: Macmillan Publishing Co., 1952), 19.

66. Michael Ruse, "Evolutionary Theory and Christian Ethics: Are They in Harmony?" 20.

67. Ibid., 21.

68. Lewis, 23.

69. Lewis, 24.

70. Ibid., 45.

71. Frank Turek, "Frank Discusses Morality with Atheist; Atheist Gives Surprising Response," crossexamined.org.

72. Lewis, 21.

73. Richard Dawkins, "Don't Force Your Religious Beliefs Own Your Children," *Time*, February 19, 2015.

74. King, Bill. "Thomas Aquinas On the Metaphysical Problem of Evil." *Quodlibet Journal* 4, no. 2 (Summer 2002): 119. This is a secondary reference for Aquinas' quote in *Compendium Theologiae*, 19.

75. Geisler, *Baker Encyclopedia of Christian Apologetics*, 224.

76. Geisler, Norman and Joseph Holden. *Living Loud: Defending Your Faith* (Nashville: B & H Publishing, 2002), 89.

77. Geisler, *Baker Encyclopedia of Christian Apologetics*, 224.

78. Ibid.

79. Ibid, 222.

80. "Bruce Little Transcript," Apologetics 315.

81. "John of God," johnofgod.com.

82. Ibid.

83. Ibid.

84. Mackie, 19-20.

85. Francis Darwin, *The Life and Letters of Charles Darwin* (London: John Murray, 1887), 1, 308.

86. "This Day in History: Salk Announces Polio Vaccine," history.com.

87. William Adams, *An Essay in Answer to Mr. Hume's Essay On Miracles*, 2nd ed. (London: Millar, Whiston, White, and Dodsley, 1754), 13.

88. C.S. Lewis, *Miracles* (New York: Macmillan Publishing Co., 1969), 13.

89. Ibid.

90. Geisler, *Baker Encyclopedia of Christian Apologetics*, 451.

91. Ayman S. Ibrahim, "Did Muhammad Perform Miracles?" First Things, September 8, 2015.

92. *Qur'an: Sahih International Translation*, under "Surah 29:51."

93. A. Godlas, "Hadith and the Prophet Muhammad," Islamic Studies, 2003.

94. Ibrahim.

95. David Alan Black, *New Testament Textual Criticism: A Concise Guide* (Grand Rapids: Baker Academic, 1994), 12.

96. Ibid., 18.

97. Justin Taylor, "An Interview with Daniel B. Wallace On the New Testament Manuscripts," March 21, 2012.

98. Brian Auten, "Daniel B. Wallace Interview Transcript," Apologetics 315, June 26, 2013.

99. "Is the New Testament Lost? Bart Ehrman vs. Daniel Wallace" (video), February 1, 2012.

100. Ibid.

101. Paul D. Wegner, *A Student's Guide to Textual Criticism of the Bible: Its History, Methods and Results* (Downers Grove, IL: IVP Academic, 2006), 25.

102. "Is the New Testament Lost?"

103. Ibid.

104. Taylor.

105. Taylor.

106. "Is the New Testament Lost?"

107. Denny Burk, "Possible First-Century Copy of Mark's Gospel Discovered," January 19, 2015.

108. "Is the New Testament Lost?"

109. J. Warner Wallace, *Cold-Case Christianity* (Colorado Springs: David C. Cook, 2013), 229.

110. Ibid., 225.

111. Ibid., 226.

112. Ibid, 226.

113. Ibid., 227.

114. Ibid., 228.

115. Bart Ehrman, "Bart Ehrman's Final Reply, The New Testament Gospels Are Not Historically Accurate," The Best Schools.

116. Ibid.

117. Ibid.

118. Ibid.

119. David Alan Black, Southeastern Baptist Theological Seminary New Testament extension course, Fall 2001. Also see Black's 2013 book, *The Authorship of Hebrews: The Case for Paul.*

120. David Alan Black, *Why Four Gospels? the Historical Origins of the Gospels* (Grand Rapids: Kregel, 2001), 35.

121. Ibid., 41.

122. Ibid., 38.

123. Ibid., 41.

124. Ibid., 37-38.

125. Ibid. 37-41.

126. Ibid., 38.

127. Ibid., 39.

128. Ibid., 38.

129. Ibid., 39.

130. Ibid., 38-41

131. Bruce Metzger, *The Canon of the New Testament: Its Origin, Development, and Significance* (Oxford: Oxford University Press, 1987), 191.

132. Michael D. Marlowe, *The Muratorian Fragment* (2001).

133. Bart D. Ehrman, *Forged: Writing in the Name of God—Why the Bible's Authors Are Not Who We Think They Are* (New York: HarperOne, 2011), 93.

134. Daniel Wallace, "1 Corinthians: Introduction, Argument and Outline," bible.org.

135. Ehrman, *Forged*, 93.

136. Marlowe.

137. F.F. Bruce, *The Canon of the New Testament, Chapter 3 in the New Testament Documents: Are They Reliable?* 5th ed. (Intervarsity Press: Leicaster, 1959).

138. Marlowe.

139. Ehrman, "Final Reply."

140. Darwin, 308.

141. F.F. Bruce, *The New Testament Documents: Are They Reliable*, 5th ed. (Stellar Books, 2013), 75, Amazon Kindle edition.

142. Ehrman, *Forged*, 208

143. Sir William Ramsay, *St. Paul the Traveler and the Roman Citizen* (Online Christian Library, 2000), 18.

144. Ibid., 12

145. John D. Davis, *The New Schaff-Herzog Encyclopedia of Religious Knowledge*, ed. Phillip Schaff (Christian Classics Ethereal Library, 2004), 8:384-87.

146. Nikos Kokkinos, "The Honorand of the Titulus Tiburtinus: C. Sentius Saturninus?" *Zeitschrift Für Papyrologie Und Epigraphik* 105 (1995): 21-36.

147. W.M. Ramsay, "Ch. 11: Quirinius, Governor of Syria," in *Was Christ Born in Bethlehem? A Study On the Credibility of St.* (n.p.: Christian Classics Ethereal Library, publication year), accessed September 27, 2016.

148. Craig Blomberg, *The Historical Reliability of John's Gospel: Issues and Commentary* (Downer's Grove: InterVarsity Press, 1987), 285.

149. Paul N. Anderson, "Aspects of Historicity in the Gospel of John: Implications for Investigations of Jesus and Archaeology," *Faculty Publications - College of Christian Studies. Paper 95* (2006): 592.

150. Ehrman, "Final Reply."

151. Norman Geisler, "Were the Gospel Writers Reporting or Creating the Words of Christ? Photo Model or Portrait Model," normangeisler.com, April 15, 2015.

152. Ibid.

153. Sir William Ramsay, *St. Paul*, 12.

154. Todd M. Compton, "Prologue," in *In Sacred Loneliness: The Secret Wives of Joseph Smith* (Salt Lake City: Signature Books, 1997).

155. Joseph Smith, *The History of the Church of Jesus Christ of Latter Day Saints* (Internet Archives), 6:408-409.

156. J.W. Wallace, 229.

157. Ibid.

158. F.F. Bruce, *The New Testament Documents: Are They Reliable*, 5th ed. (Stellar Books, 2013), 75, Amazon Kindle edition.

159. Bruce, 76. (Located in Flavius Josephus, *Josephus: The Complete Work—Jewish Antiquities* (Christian Classics Ethereal Library, under "18.5.2."

160. Bruce, 75. (Josephus, 18.3.3).

161. Bruce, 78-79.

162. Ibid., 79.

163. Ibid., 82.

164. Ibid., 84.

165. Ibid., 81.

166. Ibid., 84

167. Ibid., 81.

168. "Caesarea Maritima," Bibleplaces.com.

169. "Siloam Pool: Where Jesus Healed the Blind Man," Bible History Daily, December 3, 2015.

170. Herodotus, *The Histories*, ed. A.D. Godley, under "1.128.2."

222

171. Vassilios Tzaferis, "A Tomb in Jerusalem Reveals the History of Crucifixion and Roman Crucifixion Methods," Bible History Daily, July 22, 2011.

172. Ibid.

173. "Nazareth: Excavation of a Village House in Nazareth," Bible Archaeology, December 21, 2009.

174. "Caiaphas Bones: Tomb May Hold the Bones of Priest Who Judged Jesus," New York Times, August 14, 1992.

175. Dr. Black wrote this note on an exegetical paper I wrote on John 1:1-5, and he also discussed this interpretive issue in our New Testament class, 2001.

176. Daniel Mann, "Jesus: The Begotten of the Father," Christian Research Institute.

177. Ibid.

178. Richard R. Melick, Colossians 1:15-18, in *New American Commentary: Philippians, Colossians, Philemon* (Broadman & Holman, 1991), Logos Bible Software.

179. Ibid.

180. Ibid.

181. Wayne Jackson, "Who Is the Mysterious Shiloh," *Christian Courier.*

182. Edna Ellison, Kimberly Sowell, and Tricia Scribner, *Major Truths from the Minor Prophets: Power, Freedom, and Hope for Women* (Birmingham: New Hope Publishers, 2013), 91-101.

183. Ibid.

184. Ibid., 159-167.

185. "Jesus Christ," in *Insight*, 2:52-72.

186. "Sea of Galilee," in *Eerdman's Dictionary of the Bible*, ed. David Noel Freedman (Grand Rapids: Eerdman's Publishing Co., 2000), 1002.

187. "What's Special About the Sea of Galilee," Christian Answers.

188. Craig Blomberg. *New American Commentary: Matthew* (B & H Publishing, 1992), Logos Bible Software.

189. *The Qur'an.*

190. Geisler and Turek, *12 Points*, 27.

191. Geisler, Baker Encyclopedia of Christian Apologetics, 651-670.

192. Ibid.

193. David Alan Black, New Testament course notes.

194. Geisler, *Baker Encyclopedia of Christian Apologetics*, 80-85.

195. Geisler and Turek, *I Don't Have Enough Faith to Be an Atheist*, 364-365.

196. Geisler, *Baker Encyclopedia of Christian Apologetics*, 28-36.

197. Ibid.

198. Ibid.

199. Tricia Scribner, *Unity in Diversity: Rising Above Our Differences* (Birmingham: New Hope Publishers, 2005), 46-48. Excerpt.

200. Ibid.

201. Robert E. Coleman, *The Master Plan of Evangelism* (Grand Rapids: Fleming H. Revell), 41.

202. Edna Ellison and Tricia Scribner, *Woman to Woman: Preparing Yourself to Mentor*, (Birmingham: New Hope Publishers), 1999.

203. Chuck Colson, "Reaching the Pagan Mind," The Colson Center, November 9, 1992.

204. Clifford N. Lazarus, "Live Well: Simple Keys to Communication," *Psychology Today*, July 26, 2011.

Made in the USA
Middletown, DE
04 February 2017